LOVE

FREELY

LIVE

FULLY

AND MAKE YOUR LIFE
SPECTACULAR

JOHANNE RUTLEDGE

LOVE FREELY LIVE FULLY

Tradepaper ISBN: 978-0-578-79842-4
E-book ISBN:
Audiobook ISBN:

This book is dedicated to you.

May you be blessed for seeking awareness, and joy,

Thus, creating brighter tomorrows for all.

LOVE FREELY LIVE FULLY

Contents

LOVE FREELY LIVE FULLY

INTRODUCTION

My name is Johanne Rutledge. I am a mediumship counselor, a channeler and a humble servant of the Life Source.

I believe that 'we the people' are connected to an infinite Life Source of knowledge and wisdom. I believe that we possess all the questions and answers within us. I believe that we are powerful beings confused and lost because we are away from home.

I was told 30 years ago through guidance that I was meant to write a book. I began many times but what could I give the world that had not been already said and done.

Then the voices within came to me, year after year, revealing themselves and entrusting me with their awareness. This is how this book came about. I finally understood that I didn't have to say anything. I only had to be a clear and neutral channel for Master Souls, angels, and guides to speak up.

My entire spiritual and healing journey brought me to this exact purpose. It has been a long road where a panel of my cherished students spent hours questioning the different entities coming forth inside of me, to give us answers from a higher realm. There have been many choosing to come forward according to their expertise and desire to help humanity, sometimes to our utmost surprise.

We call them Master Souls. *Love Freely, Live Fully and Make Your Life Spectacular* has been dictated and inspired by them. I hope that you will find comfort and peace of mind through their gift of enlightenment.

PROLOGUE

I heard a great speaker say: "What I am going to tell you now, you must have heard many times, but today, it might be the right time, different wording, same message, and you will think that you are hearing it for the first time. It finally resonates with you." Are you ready to hear about what life is all about? Today might just be the day that the words suddenly make sense and hit home.

Personally, I am ready to share the meaning of life as I have been told by hundreds of souls who crossed over and through channeling thousands of hours in order to get a clear understanding for myself.

Life on Earth is simple and intricate at the same time. It all depends on where we stand. Bear with me and let us imagine that you believe in reincarnation. Let us pretend that you are in the spirit world, between lives. From a higher perspective, you are shown a complex maze as if you were a cute little mouse. At the end of the maze, is a large piece of smelly cheese which will be your prize. Looking at the maze from above, you have no fear and no doubt that it will be a 'piece of cake' to go through it gloriously in no time and make it to the prize. You excitedly accept the challenge. The other part of the bargain is that you have some past life karma to revisit and bring to closure. So, you pick some friends from your soul family and ask them to, once in a while, throw some obstacles in front of you, so you can work on a few things. You might need to grow patience, forgiveness, self-love, self-esteem, etc.

Then you find yourself in a heavy human body, standing at the entrance of the maze, and all you can see is the threshold and the first wall going nowhere in front of you. What now?

This is life on Earth in a nutshell. It is entirely a free will choice and not some kind of imposition where we are dropped off without a map or a GPS on

PROLOGUE

a strange planet where we don't belong and for no good reason at all. We signed up for the trip, we prepared for the challenges ahead and we have a plan. We are equipped with a GPS and a strong Wi-Fi connection, called higher self, to rely on each step of the way. What can go wrong?

LOVE FREELY LIVE FULLY

LOVE, ACCEPTANCE, HAPPINESS AND JOY

As soon as we are born into the flesh, we are in pursuit for what we call love. This insatiable hunger for love defines the beginning of our life and the completeness we experience at the end of our passage on Earth.

Everything we do is to sustain and grow love or shut down once hurt by love. We evaluate our worth according to the amount of love we receive from childhood and thereafter. Insufficient amount of love and approval leaves us either unable to grow self-esteem or molds us into skeptical individuals as far as love is concerned. Smothering parental love, on the other hand, may either leave us suffocated wondering why love feels like a trap or taking love for granted. The misconception of love will set the path to difficult relationship to come.

As much as we assume that love is an emotion that takes us daily on a rollercoaster, love is in fact a pure essence. This essence is who we are at the core, which always manifests itself in the energetic aura surrounding us. The first contact we have with anyone is by our aura entering a room seconds before our physical body. It announces who we are to the world, as clearly as a billboard on the highway. Therefore, our aura projects to others the level of love and value we grant to ourselves. The energy surrounding us, like a magnet, will attract its counterpart. It is why, first and foremost, we need to love ourselves. Our level of self-love indicates to others the love we expect, acknowledge, and agree we deserve. This is the hardest challenge we encounter on Earth. Bypassing the acceptance of self-love and trying to fix others instead will unfold a harder journey than necessary for the soul's evolution.

LOVE, ACCEPTANCE, HAPPINESS AND JOY

Ultimately, the purpose of each incarnation is to master self-love growing from self-acceptance.

Acceptance, happiness, and joy are three components of the essence of love.

Love begins with acceptance. If we harshly find judgment and condemnation toward our own flaws and imperfections, we will despise the same unacceptable behaviors within others. Like magnets, we will be surrounded with people mirroring what we hate about our personality or what we are afraid of becoming through DNA inheritance. In other words, we will draw to us people who demonstrate attributes that we cannot stand. Their particular traits will act as triggers of anger, fear or disgust from past experiences that have been suppressed and continue to fester. The result will be our life's dynamic constantly taking us to the same painful ending.

Acceptance is acknowledging that we chose the circle of life we are born in and the traits and aptitudes inherent to our soul brought forward from past lives. Acceptance begins with embracing who we are and initiating our transformative journey from anywhere we stand, at any age, in any circumstance and moving forward.

Acceptance in relation to those we cherish means investigating the reasons why we feel the need to change or fix them. Is it about changing what they are mirroring about our own intolerable behavior? Can it be that we are expert in suppressing feelings and controlling emotions, thus we cannot stand weaknesses in another? Again, and again, if we are unforgiving with our shortcomings and limitations, we will be uncompromising with anyone else's, especially the ones who will forgive us over and over.

However, in circumstances where we are mentally, emotionally, or physically abused by another, acceptance takes a different meaning. It means being able to still love the person while rejecting their non-acceptable behavior and distancing ourselves from any unhealthy situation. The acceptance here means to eventually give forgiveness without remaining in a permanent state of anger, resentment, or guilt. Such

4

feelings would only reduce our own capacity for a new love and bring us into repeatedly attracting the same relationship dynamic.

All experiences and lessons, no matter how hard they are, have been previously chosen and planned by us for soul evolution purpose. We have free will about the response and attitude we choose to adopt when confronted with obstacles in our daily lives; therefore, we ought to be gratefully looking upon every opportunity for growth.

This might sound idealistic, impossible, and mostly abstract amid going through physical and emotional trauma and despair. Nonetheless, that is the journey to understanding love as the ultimate goal of repetitive incarnations. Each soul must progressively become a sole representation and carrier of love. The essence of love has no boundaries and cannot be quantified or graded according to some logical measurement. If we could grasp this concept entirely and have a realization of what pure love is, we wouldn't have to be born in the flesh. In the pursuit of finding pure love, we go through ups and downs and try to love one person more exclusively than another. When the soul has progressed enough on its journey, it will realize that love is not merely an emotion initiated solely from one person, but a pure state of being. Ultimately, the soul longs to experience love in oneness with all that exist.

There are special moments given to us to get in touch with the essence of love so we may identify what it feels like. When watching a little puppy or a kitten barely able to stand up on his legs, falling and awkwardly getting up again melts our heart away, this is the pure essence of love. This puppy is not doing or giving anything to us but a moment of pure awe. When a sleeping newborn brings us to tears because it is absolute and innocent, it is connecting us to our essence of love. When nature takes our breath away with its lush green grass, sweet-smelling flowers, majestic mountains, and endless blue skies, it connects us to all that exists and to our essence. Nothing is taken and nothing is given, it just is.

LOVE, ACCEPTANCE, HAPPINESS AND JOY

This concept of love might be easier to comprehend knowing that we were created by God or the Life Source through the purest essence of love. Think of it as if we had 300 or 400 lives on Earth and we finally got down to the pure essence of love without any conditions attached. What we call unconditional love means that love would be conditional to begin with. But God, or the Life Source, has mastered it. He invented it. He created us through pure love, unconditionally.

Once, every soul that existed was one with that essence of love. Nothing else existed as "all there is" was entirely unified. Then, parts of this essence wished to experience their knowing, so humans and the Earth were created as well as other planets and beings for that purpose. There will be a time when we will graduate from the dense human experience to a state of knowing. The rollercoaster of emotions would no longer be necessary, and we will merge permanently with the essence of love once more.

Meanwhile, while in the physical body, we ought to be feeling grateful for every moment and event that brings us closer to the essence of love.

Happiness is an extension of love. A fever, a runny nose and such, are by-products of a cold, as happiness is a by-product of love. Cultivating happiness brings us closer to the essence of love. It is having a smile on our face that we can't get rid of without a reason. It is the urge to sing and dance and feeling so cheerful inside that we wish for everyone to be happy around us. The emphasis here is feeling ecstatic just to be alive with no particular motive. This is genuine happiness. It is not because we bought something, we got our dream job or we won the lottery, it's uncontrollably coming from deep inside.

Happiness is a precursor to health and brings life energy into us. It is as if a magic wand touched each and every part of our body making it function in perfect harmony. It's like drinking a health potion. When we look around us, we realize that happy people smile a lot. We can feel their life energy moving and vibrating high around them even when they are quiet. Even if we don't see it, we feel it. It's incredibly attractive. When we wish to be around a person a lot and we don't know why, it's because they are happy, and it feels uplifting to bathe in their energy. Happiness can also make some people uncomfortable, being annoyed by a feeling they do not share or understand.

If we remember the story of Peter Pan, he could only fly when he was intensely happy. It refers to those moments of happiness and lightness almost giving us wings.

Living the physical experience is not a fairy tale and it often feels more like an ongoing tragedy. Why innocent children must be sick and sometimes die or go through horrible abuse, for example, feels senseless and unbearable. From a human point of view, the mere idea of a defenseless child suffering or being tormented and deprived of their innocence and free will is incomprehensible. Spiritually, from the soul perspective, there are multiple possible reasons as to why children have to handle great challenges and pain. Only their soul knows what was agreed on before they incarnated into the body. It might be for their own growth or for their parents to develop compassion and strength, ultimately becoming an inspiration and support to others going through the same hardship. Whatever the difficulties a soul chose for its evolution, a support is also given. It might be parents, siblings or a pet that gives the child unconditional love. It allows a child to stay in the moment, grateful for every minute instead of worrying about the future. It might also be, especially in children, an inherent sense of knowing and believing in something powerful working through them. Therefore, the mind, body and soul are thankfully embracing each day as a gift never to be taken for granted. It keeps the child in a higher vibration which is conducive and necessary to healing. There's so much to be understood within a physical incarnation that only time might bring clarity and solace. Each soul's incarnation has a life plan and purpose with a contract between the soul and the soul's history. It is based on karma and the level of evolution of the soul who will tackle more challenging experiences as it grows in awareness and at higher level of consciousness. If the life chosen is filled with unimaginable obstacles, the soul has decided before birth that it had the strength and wisdom to go through it. For this soul, it was the right journey to better itself.

Does it ever occur to us that we seldom pay attention to happy events? Happy stories do not make the news. As much as we feel sad, powerless and enraged about devastating events, it is also imperative to be appreciative for people who are healthy, who get healed, and for the miracles happening every day. People fall in love, bring new babies into the world, create art and music, and save other people's lives in all kinds of ways. Yet we hardly ever hear or acknowledge this reality which energetically throws the planet out of balance. Energy is alive and as real as the air we breathe and equally as invisible. When

11

we, along with others, zero in on one particular piece of bad news, we're feeding and increasing the fear and anger energy on the Earth. If we could upload all that's going wrong, and, all that's going right into a computer, we would realize that there is also plenty of goodness and light in the world. When we mention good things instead of horrible ones happening, we might be perceived as heartless and selfish dreamers. Focusing on the positive and the beauty in the world doesn't equal to selfishness, it's merely choosing to bring and sustain the light against the dark. So it isn't about ignoring what is, it's about seeing and shedding light on all there is. We might hear on the news that a man was unjustifiably murdered and it feels unforgiveable. This man who was killed might have his own contract with life about making a difference. He might have given his lungs, heart and eyes to save three lives and brought joy and light into the world. This is the balance between light and dark. It's about understanding karma and life choices, which is extremely challenging in the physical body.

LOVE, ACCEPTANCE, HAPPINESS AND JOY

Joy is an extension of love; it is quiet and still. We have to seek joy to find it. It is found in the accumulation of happiness moments which can last from minutes to hours, and from days to weeks at a time, to eventually become joy. It is imperative to get in the practice of looking for happy instances every day. We must become aware of what triggers those moments of intimate perfection within us as well and pay attention when we unexpectedly feel light and connected to the rest of the universe. Let's notice those precious occurrences which are not conditional on anything external like an object, a person, money or power. Seeking different avenues in order to understand what our soul is longing for is a winning formula. Thinking back about our childhood let's ask ourselves what we were passionate about, what we played with for hours on end, and what made us feel on top of the world. We should hold on to this feeling and seek events, circumstances or hobbies bringing us the same joy. It will take time and practice until we easily come into the awareness of joy without any external stimulus. This is the goal and the destination. The ultimate gift for our soul is being in the essence of joy at all times.

For many of us, it seems easier to attempt making others happy other than ourselves. So we try often in vain to fix other's pain or lack of joy without lasting success. As much as we love our spouses, children and friends, we should first and foremost strive to be a source of joy as we cannot give what we don't have plenty of without quickly becoming totally depleted. In order to be a wellspring and inspiration of joy for others, it is necessary to faithfully seek our way to the essence of joy. This way, we will be enabling others to witness and comprehend what they are looking for. Showing the way is how we can help the most.

In retrospect, acceptance is the first stage for us toward fulfilment. Happiness is momentary, going from a moment to hours to days. It fluctuates in intensity from low to remarkably high to low again and is often challenging to keep in a steady vibration. Joy will come after an extended time of sustained happiness vibrations that eventually transforms into joy. Being in the essence of joy long enough will keep us in the essence of love. It's progressive and, there's no one-fits-all recipe to find and stay connected to our essence of joy. We all come from different roads and highways, different karma, and life choices. No one can pretend to tell us that there's one way to total acceptance, constant happiness, complete joy, or the everlasting essence of love. It is a way of life that works through self-awareness. It is about experiencing and staying attuned with what our soul longs for, whether it is through prayer, meditation, volunteering, keeping a healthy balance with exercise, good food, through a loving relationship or pursuing our dreams and purpose.

It is our responsibility alone to find our way to self-love which leads to love in its entirety. We would be letting life pass us by while waiting for someone to save us or bring us answers that are already lying within us. Love is the journey.

LOVE FREELY LIVE FULLY

2

KARMA

For many of us, the term Karma often resonates as a negative omen or some form of punishment. Karma, which in the ancient language of Sanskrit means action, is simply the reaction to our actions. It is like a boomerang returning to the sender. Seeds that were sowed in our past lives as well as in the present become the trail toward our destiny. Like a rock creating ripples once thrown into a lake, our attitudes and reactions to life challenges reverberate.

Karma is neither good nor bad. If our path is difficult to begin with, let's realize that we created it that way before our incarnation in order to learn teachings not yet understood. Karma is based on behaviors and decisions made earlier in this life and/or in past lives. Basically, each lifetime is the ultimate chance for us to become the greatest version of what we are meant to be, based on our soul's purpose. We chose that purpose and decided on its road map to follow before birth, so it is about remembering. Through following our intuition, listening to the little voice inside, connecting to God or the Life Source and to our higher self, we can tap into the information necessary to stay on the chosen path.

Unfortunately, when we get away from our connection to the Life Source and from our soul's desires, we begin considering the body merely as a physical vehicle. The soul then inhabits the body while solely engrossed in the physical experience. Once we have lost sight of our life's purpose, the very reason we came here in the first place, we no longer know where we are heading. From that point on, it's easy to see how we can get caught up in creating more arduous karma than resolving them.

KARMA

Whenever we harm ourselves or another being, it will affect all of us in this world that we share. Every emotion felt, whether it is compassion, joy and gratitude or envy, anger and resentment will grow and ripple endlessly as energy is shared throughout the world. Thoughts are also made of energy and travel fast. Negative energy vibrations from thoughts and words are limitless in space and time. When we contemplate negative thoughts toward another, someone else will have hurtful thoughts toward us. The result might be for us to feel sad, depressed, hurt or guilty without any plausible cause. The goal is to experience what it feels like to receive what we send to others. If negative thoughts are sent our way without a legitimate reason and we're mostly filled with love and joy within, it will bounce back to the sender right away. This is karma.

Whatever we do, think or say consistently will eventually be attracted into our life dynamic by cause and effect. When we keep complaining about our job every day saying, "I'm so tired of this job", we might wish to get fired and collect unemployment. It might not be how the universe will respond to us whining. If we say, "I'm sick and tired of this job", the universe might just make us sick and tired with an illness that will stop us from attending to any work at all. It would be the same principle when we say, "I hate this old car" which might bring us to wrecking the car in an accident where we might end up seriously hurt. Let's be aware of our words and not use a negative when we wish for a positive change. We don't know how karma is going to manifest itself in our life. Again, it is not a form of punishment but a wake-up call to the realization that we create our own reality through repetitive thoughts and words.

It might seem like a lot of work to constantly monitor what we think and say, but in fact it's about making different choices and gradually changing our way of expressing our wishes and desires. For example, if we're not happy with our job anymore, we might say, "I'm grateful for my work, but I'll be happier with this other particular kind of job that better suits me and that I will enjoy much more." Saying it and most importantly, feeling it as if it was already ours, is the key to the new job manifestation. The universe responds well to positive and confident commands. Then trust, and see miracles happen. Thoughts materialize with time. Stick to it no matter how long it takes. Whatever we put out, we will harvest. We are that powerful.

We can rest assured that the universe has a way to bring us back on track if we keep missing the hints and repeat the same debilitating patterns over and over again. In the midst of emotional situations, it is difficult to recognize the behaviors and choices that attract to us the same hurtful outcome. The respect, the level of appreciation, and the self-love we give ourselves for being who we are, is exactly what we will receive from everyone else. If we have been wronged, bullied or cheated on in many ways and disrespected or taken for granted, it is time to take a long look in the mirror. We can't point the finger outward and play victim when in reality, deep down, we don't believe in deserving better. We need to change our thoughts and perception of who we are.

Some of us might think that doing good deeds and helping others is adding points into a good deed account as a way of feeling more deserving. It doesn't work that way. First and foremost, it is about getting to be up close and personal with our soul, willingly and thoroughly understanding what we are made of. We must be grateful for our assets while working on healing our fears, weaknesses and downfalls. This alone will grow our self-love and our self-acceptance. We are then empowered and equipped to love, help, and support others which will bring us joy. When we leave the Earth and go back home, we will look back and see the positive impact we have done. It will enable us to love, accept and forgive ourselves for mistakes or mishaps. By the law of karma, the love we spread will come right back to us. Let's remember that any act of selfless love has to be done with a pure and caring intention and not simply because it's either the right thing to do, through guilt or for recognition. The law of karma cannot be transmuted.

Whether we harm ourselves or others it will create karma. For example, terminating pregnancy causes karma, as every decision we make will have a consequence. It's neither positive nor negative; it's an experience. When we consider abortion, multiple reasons may have brought such a decision. A contract might have been made with a soul before the mother and child were born. The two souls might have agreed that in time, the soul would come to the mother for a short period in the hope of opening her heart to unconditional love. It could be that the mother's health would be endangered or that the baby might be born gravely disabled, making it the parent's decision to terminate the pregnancy. It could be that a woman's life conditions may be very difficult and she feels that it isn't a safe environment for the baby or herself. There are also instances when abortion is used as contraception. Each abortion creates karma or "cause and effect" as karma is not a punishment but an opportunity to learn about consequences following our intentions and choice of actions. Souls within the human body evolve through experiences, some easier than others.

Karma might be that we are driving and caused an accident, and someone got hurt. We might have not been paying attention to the road, driving carelessly or driving impaired. There will be karma following according to how we react to the situation. If we are really deeply sorry, acknowledge our mistake, and do whatever it takes to redeem ourselves, the karmic lesson might be assimilated. If we blame it on others and keep the same driving behavior, we will create a similar situation to happen to us or to a loved one in this life time or in the next. The universe's response is not always what we might expect for us to integrate the experience. We have to remember that we brought this accident in our life for a growth purpose in the first place. The person who got badly hurt brought forth this experience in her or his life, as well, for a purpose that they should eventually realize. If they forever hold anger, resentment and carry a grudge against us, it will be their part of the karma to understand. Accidents are not random and, as horrible as it may seem, it is often a contract between two souls. There are hundreds of scenarios and life contracts possible. It could be that we are not paying attention to life's signs while moving toward goals totally opposite to our purpose or highest good in life. We can be taking life for granted, carelessly threatening our health or destiny, so the universe might bring us to a stop, often physical, as in illness or an accident. Therefore, when an accident occurs, that person has the choice to hate us or take her share of responsibility and forgive with time. Everything that happens to us is a wake-up call. There is also the possibility that one person is seriously injured or dies to offer a second chance at life to the other individual who will make it a life's goal to raise awareness on driving safely. Nothing is pure coincidence. There's a purpose to absolutely every event whether it's for us or the other person involved. When something happens, it's an opportunity to wonder what the lesson is or what we have been incessantly thinking about.

Karma also applies to Mother Earth. We humans sometimes think that we can keep taking from people, from life and from Mother Earth without consequences. For millions of years, the planet has been working at replenishing itself, but just like body parts, organs and cells, it gets used up. It gets to a point where a body cannot be repaired anymore and we need a new one. Mother Earth is tired and she is getting more and more depleted every day. She can hardly cleanse or filter herself anymore as her natural filters are getting destroyed. The human race came up with so many devastating forces that she is running out of resources. I was shown a time where earth will be 85% depleted, with only 15% of the planet able to clean and restore itself. I saw that the next 25 years are going to bring a lot more destruction. Earth will have to go to great lengths to stay alive.

The karma of destruction and gigantic natural disasters has already begun all over the planet. If we don't make quick changes, the planet won't allow itself to be destroyed and will do whatever it takes for survival. There will be a lot more rain. As long as the Earth can filter itself through oceans, rivers and lakes, it will keep the planet going. There will be a time when water will take over much of the land.

Humanity is alive because Mother Earth sustains life by giving us air, food, and water. We think that we're in control of the planet but without her there is nothing; we can't exist. We're taking for granted what maintains our existence. We need to stop depleting and restoring instead. There was a time where we could have done it a little step at a time, but those days are gone. Drastic measures have to be taken first and foremost by large industries. They should cooperate and show the way! They must get involved because it is the right karmic way to use their important influence in the world. Don't pollute the water and the air. Don't make more garbage than necessary. Grow things, which is what the Earth is good at! We need to work with what the Earth is giving us, support what she does and aim to keep proper balance between taking and giving.

When it comes to finding a global resolution, while some of us are already very committed about the Earth's balance, others don't yet comprehend the seriousness of the planet's distress. Getting angry, resentful, and violent against those who are not yet believing in the reality of the Earth's despair, will only bring more unbalance into the planet. We cannot be forced into changing or adopting a new behavior unless we clearly understand why and realize the impact of the problem on our own day-to-day life. Once we can apply a new philosophy of living to our own back yard and lives, it will talk to our heart, not only to our logical minds. We are told why plastic bottles are detrimental to the planet. When plastic burns, it poisons the very air we breathe and it destroys the oceans. This is only one of our realities right here, right now. We're responsible for it. This is what needs to be said, taught and shown especially to kids in school so they can educate their parents, again touching their heart.

When it comes to Mother Earth, this is one of the strongest karmic consequences there is because it involves all humanity's survival. We have heard the expression "you have made your bed so now lay in it." It means we must work with what we created. Mother Earth is our vessel, she allows us to experience life. Because we mistreated her, we will struggle with the consequences. It is direct karma.

It is not useful to live in fear of the future. On the other hand, it's highly necessary to begin living in full awareness of what life is all about. Karma is not a fearful or terrible word. We have a tendency to jokingly say "oh, it must be karma." In fact it is, but it can be fun or it can be challenging. Karma is only a response to an experience from which to take responsibility and evolve. Karma is why we came back in a human body to embrace.

LOVE FREELY LIVE FULLY

3

LIFE'S PURPOSE

Finding out our life's purpose, when we embark in yet another Earth expedition, is the reason we keep moving forward, rain or shine. We hope that each incarnation will bring us closer to total consciousness which is the highest level of soul evolution. Such evolution is based on how wisely we integrate experiences, lessons, and challenges. They are for us to realize that life's ups and downs are a gift of awareness. Ideally, we will then begin to relate to each other's hardships. As we evolve, we may be guiding others on how to leap over obstacles, becoming light workers or carriers of light.

In between lives, in the spirit world, we reunite with our soul family. Before each incarnation, we voluntarily signed up with souls we love and care about, and with whom we experienced previous lives and karma. We partner with members of our soul family for mutual support and growth before beginning our next round of physical passage on Earth.

The souls that join us in each of our sojourns on the Earth do not belong to us. They simply willingly take some of their given time on the planet to fulfill a purpose in our life's script as well as in their own. They may play the role of a lover, a spouse, a parent, sibling, child, pet or any other friend that impacts our life. Our soulmates accept to come again into our lives to help us open up our heart, learn virtues such as forgiveness, courage, compassion and patience, and support us during painful growth periods. We ought to consider as a teacher, each and every soulmate crossing our path. We should feel grateful for the lesson, no matter how difficult. Once we have bonded with another's energy, the bond will not be broken unless one of the two decides to cut the energetic cords. Because we are emotional beings, we have a tendency to own things, pets, people and even time. All is only given to us as tools for the soul evolution and not for a power struggle.

When it is time for each of our soulmates to part from us for any reason, let's not ask the Life Source why those lives were taken away from us, but ask the Life Source why in its great wisdom, it gave us this chance to feel, to learn, and to experience love as the purest essence.

The karma that we decided to revisit this time and our present choices, together with our level of fear, doubt, denial or acknowledgement when it comes to love, dictates our present life's path. It defines the depth of the love experience necessary for the soul full development. The Life Source doesn't choose or decide the script of our life, WE DO!

In our lifetime, there's room for being the most grateful person that we can be, in expending and embracing the gifts and passions that our soul carried over at birth. We may be an artist, a waitress, a doctor, a mechanic, a carpenter or a preacher, etc. Any profession or job in the world will enrich us if we embrace who we are with all the passion, devotion and gratitude that we can gather. It is important to be true to ourselves once we understand, accept and acknowledge our ideal, which is what ignites the spark within us. Our ideal is what we aim to accomplish in this lifetime because it will fill up our hearts with thankfulness and joy, sharing ourselves with the world, which is the ultimate goal. It's wasteful to spend years and decades in universities if we are not aware of our real purpose, and working toward its realization. Passion, ideal and purpose are not found within the brain but within the heart. What is our heart longing for? Most of us don't make time to ask ourselves that question. At the end of the day, the cure for sadness, depression and feelings of emptiness within is to know that we make a difference and that we are fulfilling our own prophecy. It is critical to take a break from the rat race to listen to the little voice inside that is our intuition. What we call meditation is the art of listening and be still long enough to hear the answers we're seeking. Being responsible for our choices is essential. If we feel ourselves wondering in directions not resonating with a feeling of joy, if we think or feel no passion for what we do or pride for the way we behave, it is imperative to choose again!

Most of us work to pay the bills. But our jobs or careers, often leave us feeling empty. It is our responsibility to find a hobby that will wake up a spark of joy within us, and with enough faith and perseverance, it might eventually spur us on to a different and fantastic journey. We must take the steps to make it happen no matter where, when or what we begin with. We might have just a little money or time on our hands, but interestingly enough, when it's about doing something we really like, we find the time and energy. A magic way to find joy and make a difference is volunteering. Time doesn't cost anything. When we volunteer with love and an open heart, we might just find our destiny or a new job or career opportunity. The universe does support us when we support life. We must put ourselves out there. We have love enough to spare; let's spread it and see how it feels. Everything is not tallied in a bank account. Whether we have tons of time or money or very little, the process is the same. Giving with our heart no matter what we have available is the key. We can offer freely the work we do best, spreading around an uplifting smile, or being compassionate and willing to listen quietly to someone who needs to be heard. The magic takes place by getting out of our head and focusing on our heart and trusting what makes us feel like giants.

If it is still difficult for us to find our ideal, let's look at everyday life and at what makes us giggle. What gets us excited? Let's sit down and put it on paper. What brings a smile on our lips and brings us in a day dream state? When we were children, what we played with was a window into our passion, so let's travel back in our memories, see ourselves as children again and pay attention to how we feel. Our emotions will take us to the right place, at the right time, with the right people. We will know this in our gut, which is our emotional directional barometer in life.

The process of self-discovery is simpler than we anticipated. It begins with appreciating the basic activity of sitting outside at sunrise and sundown and feeling amazed and grateful for witnessing such a miracle of beauty. Then, when we eat, making time to chew and savor every bite, being thankful for the ability to taste and feed our body as well as appreciating the opportunity to drink a glass of life-giving water. The secret is taking time to recognize every simple happy moment. Joy is a multitude of happy moments and the gratitude that comes along with it. Let's pay attention to the change slowly taking place within us. We're the first person we need to focus on, as we cannot make others happy if we completely suppress and disregard how we feel. Happiness is catching; it spreads from the inside out. Soon it turns into joy and when we hold the feeling of joy as long and as often as we can, we become a beacon of light. Once we grow our light in whatever form it may be, we begin lighting up others, paying our gratitude forward and making a difference in this world.

We are all wondering about the purpose of being on Earth, in this body, family, country and moment in time. We were totally aware of it before entering the physical body and we agreed on all the particulars, mostly based on past karma. Our responsibility is to dig within ourselves and remember it through zooming in on our passions, abilities and natural gifts no matter where we begin. Our purpose is to learn lessons and bring closure to past karma, to feel and cultivate joy, and consequently bring our contributions to the world.

4

LIFE SOURCE, HIGHER SELF, GUIDES and ANGELS

Whether we name the Creator God or Life Source or in any other way, all lives have been created by an incredible loving energy that performed the miracle of birth. There are many belief systems explaining the beginning of the human existence and it is for us to decide which one feels right. The one truth that cannot be denied is the fact that a powerful, all-knowing force created the universe for all to co-exist. God or the Life Source ultimately contains all there is in the universe, meaning that all energies reside within the Life Source.

LOVE FREELY LIVE FULLY

The Life Source embraces us unconditionally and instills in us an overwhelming desire to improve the quality of this energy that we are. We aspire to a total synthesis with the Life Source that created us. The Life Source says, "I love you in the perfection that you are". It never says that we are not good enough or not worthy to return home. We are the ones longing for more experiences, hoping to raise our awareness and heighten the vibrations of our energy.

Our higher self is the part of us that remains in the high-energy vibration inside the Life Source, while a spark of our essence incarnates into a physical body in the hopes of evolving further. In the body, we are avatars while our higher self is guiding and monitoring our voyage on the planet, using what we call our intuition. The Life Source is home while we are going away to school. Our higher self contains our essence, energy, identity and our entire evolution history. Within the Life Source, between lives, our soul together with higher guidance, review our soul's growth through incarnations. Some of our life's purposes might have not been understood and processed in a satisfactory manner to us. The outcome of our life review will determine the next karma to be addressed along with the purpose of the next incarnation. Our ultimate goal is to bring the lessons to completion and the soul to a higher degree of evolution.

We as humans might have the misconception that we are the center of the universe. Like children, we have a tendency to behave as if we and the planet are indestructible. Nothing can be further from the truth. We should be grateful and acknowledge our appreciation through caring for Mother Earth. Among the multiple reasons that the planet Earth is extremely precious is the special opportunity for growth that she gives humans, through experiencing and feeling emotions from deep despair to the highs of excitement and love.

Our higher self, which resides within the Life Source, is our GPS (global positioning system) making sure we stay on the path we have chosen. We are connected to our full essence at all times. When we feel lost and abandoned, it is mostly because of the chatter of the mind hindering the full connection to our higher self. Quieting the mind is imperative to be receptive to guidance. This means staying still long enough to grasp and acknowledge answers to our inquiries. If we pray and beg for help, we must have faith that our request will be answered. The higher self brings us answers and support in many forms. It might make us cross paths with a person who will advise us, or bring forth a song or a movie that will inspire us at a crossroads. It may even throw in a roadblock if it is necessary for us to let go of something or someone in order to find the right path. Meditation, yoga or breathwork are some examples of tools to adopt on a regular basis to quiet down an overactive and fearful mind.

In response to prayers or questions, our higher self, guides and the Life Source will often answer by bringing thoughts into our mind. Those thoughts show up out of nowhere. We call them intuition, gut feeling, or a hunch. Intuitive or sensitive individuals might pick up answers as voices talking in their mind. It is easy to discount the guidance as imagination, thinking that it is our own thoughts and creation. Listening to our guidance will never steer us wrong. Guidance might strongly suggest that we change our usual route that day, turning left instead of right, helping us avoid a car accident. Keeping track of multiple times when we refuse to follow our intuition on a small or larger scale, and subsequently remembering what happened, would bring us confirmation of such guidance. Some of us are uncomfortable when feeling thoughts of strong advice arises in our minds. The solution is to slow down and stop filling up the silence with the sound of the radio, the television or the internet. Silence is the needed space that allows our higher self and guides to connect with us and show us an easier way to fulfilment and happiness. In order to realize our purpose in the easiest way possible, it is fundamental to stay away from anything that would numb our mind such as medications, recreational drugs or alcohol; those are crutches that shut off the channel of guidance given to us as a support system.

Our minds, bodies and souls are created as perfect channels in order to receive constant directions. Once our soul acknowledges the guidance and our mind calms down long enough to receive it, we are responsible to keep the physical body in good health and balance. Our choice of nourishment should be food that agrees with our metabolism and doesn't make us feel drowsy, tired, or stuffed after a meal. It would be foolish to expect our body to digest an excessive amount of food, sometimes lacking nutrients and damaging the harmony of our body functions, and still expect the mind to be alert and receive guiding advice.

In order to support us through the Earth plane challenges, the Life Source also brings forth chosen guides to further assist us during our passage in the human body. Our guides are also part of our soul family but might remain in energy form instead of coming in physical form. Guides are devoted to helping us maneuver life's challenges as easily as possible, but they need to be asked and allowed to help. Guides might also be loved ones that have made their transition from this present lifetime. Their Earth experience might be over for now, but they might still be fulfilling their contract about loving and watching over us until we are reunited in the Life Source.

Angels also often volunteer to be our support system. In preparation for our next incarnation, our higher self may realize that this next journey might bring forth highly challenging moments and hardships. Angels who never were in the physical body will sign up for our much needed support. It is an agreement between the higher self and the angelic realms, so that they may assist when those moments occur. Imagine, for example, that you were in a car accident that was not supposed to take place. We were given guidance that we didn't listen to and the accident happened. An angel might save our life in that case, or lessen the impact. It could also be possible that we momentarily find ourselves in the depths of depression and try to take our own life. An angel could intervene, knowing that it is not our time and that it would create additional karmic debt. Angels cannot impose themselves on us, but in exceptional instances, an intervention could come about provided it's in accord with the agreed life plan before our incarnation. The understanding would be if we signed up for an experience that turned out to be very difficult, the angels may intercede. Beyond that, if we believe in angels, we may ask them to get involved in our daily pursuits. Angels will help us, when necessary, if the request is coming from a loving place, and doesn't interfere with the wisdom we should be acquiring.

Archangels are believed to be from an upper hierarchy, so more powerful than angels. They can be called upon to support and guide us in arduous times. Each archangel has their own area of influence. We can also read about them and find out which ones we resonate with the most, then ask for their assistance when necessary.

Guidance from the spirit world will manifest in our life in the most desirable manner for who we are and according to the belief system of our present lifetime and experience. It might be angels, archangels, but also gods and goddesses or masters, to name a few.

Some of us even feel more comfortable and trust animals more than people. Our guidance might show up as a bird, cat, dog, horse, or any other loving soul from the animal kingdom. Plants and flowers could also be sent into our life by our guides to remind us that spirit comes through in unexpected ways when all seems lost.

We often pray and beg for help when situations are precarious and we cannot seem to find a solution to issues or a way out of scary circumstances. Guiding signs should always light up our heart and make us feel warm and safe, sometimes bringing tears of relief and joy. Any directives that would instill in us fear and discomfort, or promote physical illness, would not be from the Life Source; it would be a reflection of our own fear. Fearfulness attracts and opens the way for earthbound spirits that are in opposition to our highest good. Earthbound spirits and entities are mostly lost souls who refused to cross into the light for various reasons after they left the body. Guides, loved ones and angels coming from the Life Source will cause us to be in awe of the seeming coincidences that took place to get us where we needed to be. Fear, along with angry thoughts, will bring advice that mirrors dark feelings that might engulf us during a particular level of hardship. Deep depression, sad emotions, and grief may prevent us from having the hope of a better tomorrow. Medications, drugs, and alcohol often add or increase a distressed state of mind until we can see no way out. As dark and scary as that state of being may be, we must find enough faith to make the decision of reaching out for help instead of slowly slipping into numbness.

We all have heard this line before, "You are never alone". Our soul is at all times connected to the Life Source. Our first step is to believe that the higher power that created us would never send us on a life journey without guidance and emergency support. Support consists of God or the Life Source, our higher self, guides, angels, loved ones who went back home and other Light energy beings that we trust. When in the midst of a situation of pain, betrayal, abandonment or doubts, a fearful reaction would be to get angry and pull away from the loving care of the Life Source because we don't want to hear and accept the lesson behind the hurt. It is a choice. Another choice would be to reach out to a friend or a therapist for us to re-evaluate our dark perception of a circumstance. Once we are able to ease up the intensity of the situation, we can return to prayers, meditation, or guidance to regain balance and peace of mind.

LOVE FREELY LIVE FULLY

Life constantly reflects our thoughts and actions to us, with an amazing precision like a boomerang returning to the sender. Being aware of this reality, what would we like to receive?

5

ADDICTIONS AND SURVIVAL

Many roads can lead to addictions. Being torn by anger, rejection and a lack of love and approval are most debilitating. But something even more sneaky and consuming may throw us into an abyss: the absence of self-love and the emptiness of not knowing where we belong, where to turn, and why we breathe and live.

An addiction is the crutch that we're craving to a point that we can no longer think or function properly unless we have it to fill the gap. An Addiction is sometimes the only thing we believe that we can control even if, in fact, it is the other way around.

LOVE FREELY LIVE FULLY

Addictions are a way to deal with a reality that doesn't seem acceptable to us. An addiction is a cushion between us and the pressure of what we do not want to deal with in our everyday life. It could be an excess of alcohol, drugs, pills, smoking, eating, self-mutilation, compulsive sex, gambling, shopping or shoplifting, exercising or working beyond healthy boundaries. Anything that will alter the now and bring us an escape. It gives us something to deal with instead of dealing with our reality. It is often passed on through cellular memory from one generation to the next. When one individual finally finds enough determination and healthy ways to handle life for what it is, the destructive cycle can be stopped before it passes on to the children and grandchildren.

Addictions are there to show us that we are out of balance in some areas of our life, or in all of them. Recognizing our painful wounds and addressing them can be truly challenging. Abandoning the safety blanket we created might be the most torturous and scary venture we will undertake but might turn out to be the most empowering ever.

Turning and returning to our thoughts in our mind day after day will not produce a different outcome. In order to understand the dynamic of our lives, we need to reach out for assistance in finding clarity and a helpful resolution. It is essential to come to terms with the fact that we each chose to come in a physical body to experience emotions, obstacles and life lessons for our soul's evolution. Being in a human body, we can understand when an addiction will show up along the way at a time when we are facing fear, uncertainty or insecurity. In order to get away from an addiction which is consuming our will and our life, no matter how hard it is, we must face the facts. Then, using our free will, a decision has to be made to drastically change the way we deal with life's challenges. It would be tough, and at times impossible, to tackle such monster habits alone. Once we decide to make a change, it's of the utmost importance to reach out for professional support and healing. It may be a person who already went through the experience and conquered it, a group or a particular therapy that will resonate with our heart and feel right. The options are between honoring our life's choices and contracts agreed upon before birth or finding excuses, feeling victimized and blaming our birth conditions, our family, our friends, society and life all together.

What we don't face now, we will face the next life around. It will not get easier next time. On the contrary, because life has to be conquered for the soul to grow, there will be more obstacles added to the course. Hard times will show up life after life until handled properly.

Some of us can fool ourselves and deny our addictions, creatively hiding them from family and friends. Obvious signs of addictive behavior of a loved one maybe when they lose their sense of priorities and balance. A personality is altered by unusual anger, distress and denial. Acknowledgment of the addiction would leave them feeling totally vulnerable.

At this point, using confrontation and telling someone that we know what their problem is means we already lost the battle. The first step is for the person to acknowledge that they need a crutch. It may be a conversation done in a loving casual way and without judgment, guiding the person into pouring their feelings out about how their addiction makes them feel. Through the person expressing how they feel, they might come to a realization on their own of what they are trying to compensate for. The next step is for the person to decide to make a change. All addictions can be addressed this way but it will most likely take a professional therapist to allow deep emotional issues to surface and be dealt with when it comes to core addictions. It's about our loved one's recognition and awareness instead of automatic response. Most of all, let's remember that we cannot be the therapist of a loved one. It would be difficult to be objective and we could be oblivious to the fact that we might be part of the problem. Give acknowledgement, but do not say "I know what you are going through" if you don't.

One of the most controversial subjects and belief systems, which we call religion, is primarily a choice and not an addiction until we are willing to punish, reject or destroy anyone who chooses differently than we do. Some of us refuse to acknowledge our own feelings, fears and life difficulties, so we devote ourselves to something else. We often take on a cause which might be religion and make it our God. We often ignore our own dilemmas as we embrace someone else's beliefs and reality. It's a strong and self-denigrating kind of addiction. It's when all of the emotions of self are in denial. We might be completely ignorant of who we are and of what we are made of because it's easier to join the crowd. Unfortunately, it is often passed on through generations until one soul decides to assert itself and make different choices.

ADDICTIONS AND SURVIVAL

The most destructive addiction of human beings is to feel defeated before even going into battle. We suffer from a lack of faith. We come to this planet to experience emotions and then we let them get the best of us. We look at the worst that can happen. The human race could be called the self-defeated race. We don't need others to knock us down because we do it all on our own. Our ego is so fearful that we don't acknowledge the flaws, weaknesses, and insecurities inherent to our humanness because it may mean not being loved or admired anymore. This is our worst issue. Addictions replace speaking up about who we are deep down, opening about the not-so-glorious sides of ourselves.

Once we master self-love and acceptance, addictions will no longer serve us, and we will earnestly embrace our life the way it was intended to be lived.

LOVE FREELY LIVE FULLY

6

HEALTH AND HEALING

Being and staying healthy is a multi-dimensional daily endeavor. As human beings, our first and most important goal by far is to achieve balance. It is essential for us to engage in our own personal search realizing that any physical disease comes from not being emotionally at ease. This will most likely require the courage to go back into our childhood memories to begin with, which is often where we made an opinion about who we are.

What made us sick in the first place was suppressing emotions such as sadness, shame, fear, anger, resentment, guilt, and low self-esteem, and it needs to be processed and released. These emotions are overwhelming and painful to face on our own. It is fundamental to reach out to a therapist or counselor to explore with us our repressed and sometimes denied gut-wrenching memories. Memories are powerful root energies subtly growing within and finally finding escape into a physical materialization. This is when the body becomes ill at any level.

Another aspect of deep-rooted emotions causing physical issues sometimes, comes from lives before our present incarnation. Identifying these issues might require the help of someone who can access and shed light on our previous lives history. At times, understanding the choices and dynamics of our past lives linked to the present one may open the door to personal forgiveness and help us come to term with confusing feelings.

Relying on professionals to help us figure out things is a great step forward toward feeling whole and happy but a large part of the healing responsibility relies on us to begin with, by way of a thorough introspection.

Writing a diary daily helps in dealing with feelings as they surface instead of burying them down. Writing our life's memoir on paper might bring the past from a foggy perception to the more truthful version of our reality.

We may also conduct our own investigation while writing down questions for ourselves such as, "How far back can I remember events in my life?" Or "Was I happy as a child?" "What made me feel safe?" "Did I feel loved?"

Research has brought forth amazing discoveries and ways to help humanity move forward. It's unfortunate that we bypass self-analyzing, the study of our own self. The past cannot be kept concealed; it will eventually turn into physical illness. A time comes when it needs to resurface to be understood, forgiven, and fully processed.

Once we become aware that inside most of us are children with broken hearts and broken minds, we understand the importance to begin healing at the earliest age possible when it comes to children.

LOVE FREELY LIVE FULLY

Once again, observing the emotional behaviors of children will indicate their hidden issues. What makes children uncomfortable or upset? What provokes anger, jealousy, or tantrums? Is the child shy, with a tendency to be isolated? There are many signs of emotional stumbling blocks, from the birth trauma itself to past-life residuals. Being aware of children's personalities and tendencies early in time gives parents the opportunity to address problems before they get out of hand. It is often a misconception to deny predicaments, thinking that things will get better with time, on their own or with medication. Again, as for adults or children, we ought to reach out for help before emotional distress turns into unhealthy and unmanageable behaviors.

Once we are fully aware and understand our life's dynamic, there are many ways to dislodge and clear trapped energies within the organs and cells of our bodies. In the physical realm, some of these ways may include chiropractic alignment, acupuncture, osteopathic alignment, massage therapy, Craniosacral therapy, various forms of yoga, Qigong, Tai Chi and many other methodologies, including some Chinese herbs linked to energy clearing. On the energetic level, methods may include professional hypnosis, regression, rebirthing, breath work, Healing Touch, Body Talk, Reiki, Theta Healing, Bars Healing, crystal healing therapy, sound therapy and shamanic healing, to name a few, as well as techniques by certain healing practitioners who use their own methods, often in conjunction with guidance from the spirit world. There are many more options to choose from. When a person is willing and ready to be helped, the right healing practitioner will come along.

Healers are individuals who channel healing energy from the Life Source. Some have better antennas for channeling because of their true, selfless intentions of wanting to help others, as well as being dedicated to clearing their own emotional baggage. Those healers are like clear crystals in the way that they are totally open to receive, get charged and move forward light and loving energy to another being. In other words, some people channel better than others depending on how they take care of themselves physically, emotionally, mentally and spiritually.

Finding the right, genuine healing practitioner can be confusing. Our first step is to follow our intuition about how this person makes us feel. Do we like their energy, feeling peaceful around them, or do we feel nervous and intimidated? We should also inquire about their background, what brought them to helping others, as well as asking them to define how they learned their particular way of healing.

It is imperative to remember that when we seek a healer, we may harbor the belief that this person will heal or fix us. In fact, it is a total misconception. The healing practitioner will allow loving energy to flow from the Life Source through them, then into us, in order to give our body the boost to heal itself. It means that the recipient is in charge of willingly receiving and working with the energy. We have to participate in our own healing, step by step, following the emotional, physical, mental, and spiritual guidance we are given. When in need and seeking help, we cannot expect a miracle to take place without efforts of our own. In reality, practitioners are not healers but merely instruments of healing.

Another component necessary for healing is to search within ourselves and make sure that we genuinely want to get back to health. Some of us are creating a disease as a crutch for various reasons. It might be an excuse for not moving forward in life because we are overwhelmed by our circumstances. On the other hand, we might be blaming our misery or misfortune on everything and everyone. Taking responsibility would mean to get out of the victim role, reach out for professional help, and conquer each challenge beginning where we are no matter how hard it seems.

Every soul is born with the gift of healing because we are coming from the same Life Source, with the power to channel its energy. In order to develop our healing birth right, we need to acknowledge and dedicate time and effort to becoming a clear channel

65

through self-clearing of our past traumas and karma. The more lives a healing practitioner has dedicated to self-healing as well as to channeling healing for others, the more their energy may expand. In this incarnation they may have to a higher level of connectiveness and synchronicity with the Life Source healing energy. If we don't connect and channel from the Life Source, we will use our own energy instead and get rapidly depleted.

In our everyday life, there are multiple ways for us to begin feeling more in tune with our inner-self. Integrating new information into our mind and soul is one of them. Uplifting affirmations can be an integral part of our regimen. They work wonders in the mirror, looking ourselves in the eye and proclaiming positive and impactful words of wisdom to ourselves. A very powerful one is to speak your name and say "I love you." It might feel ridiculous at first but it pays off to persevere. An important fact about affirmations is to realize that an affirmation is a statement. Statements are the most commanding words proclaimed to the universe and to our higher self. Affirmations manifest what we believe and state as long, as it is for our well-being. We must also realize that there is perfect timing for everything.

Working with positive affirmations is highly beneficial, although emptying out the toxic attitudes we might have cultivated is crucial. That includes criticizing and talking down to self, along with making our mission to keep up with all that's going wrong in the world. It is of prime importance to keep most of our energy focused on the way we participate in our highest good, which will reflect on the world around us.

One of the causes of emotional dis-eases on Earth is the lack of physical contact. The aging population, the sick, the loners, single or shy individuals among others, are longing for human touch. It is one of the reasons massage therapy brings healing to the mind, body and soul. Massage primarily helps the body to release pain caused by toxins accumulated in muscles. Muscle contraction also traps energy; consequently, the flow of blood and oxygen becomes limited. Massage will sometimes bring a person to tears from emotional release, a process that should be welcomed. Being aware that the energy of two people touching connects instantaneously, it is important to carefully choose a therapist performing healing of any form. We have to feel comfortable with the healing practitioner's vibrations and frequency to get a positive outcome.

Everything in existence, solid or liquid, is made of energy. Energy vibrates and creates a frequency. Humans are vibrational beings. When we encounter others and feel comfortable and happy to spend time with them, it is often because our frequencies are compatible. We normally think that this person feels very agreeable to be around. What we actually feel attracted to or put off by are their vibrations and frequency.

Humans have invented different avenues to raise their vibrations in order to emotionally feel better in their body, from soundwave machines to various drugs. As much as medication is sometimes necessary while in deep emotional distress, some people opt for drugs as the quicker and easier fix. This route only offers temporary results and nurtures co-dependency. We are powerful machines and should stop giving our power away because we are seeking nice and easy results.

In order to raise our vibrations, we need to lighten up our minds and declutter the emotional baggage weighing us down. It is essential to allow and schedule time for being in the moment. This is attainable in different ways, such as through meditation, all forms of yoga, breathwork, Qigong and Tai Chi, etc., which are great tools for raising vibrations and reconnecting with the Life Source.

Connecting with Mother Earth is an utmost and powerful way to raise vibrations as well. Spending time next to a body of water, walking in nature, lying down in the grass staring up at the sky, and wholeheartedly hugging a tree are natural ways to ground. We need to find the way that suits us the most. At first, the effect will last for a few minutes, and through practice, vibrations will stay higher for longer periods of time. We will know this through lightness and feeling a soothing sense of peace within.

Practicing conscious breathing, slowly and deeply in clean air is essential to move life energy within every cell. If the body is depleted by poor eating, smoking and drinking habits, air pollution, drugs or lack of exercise, cells are deprived of oxygen and the immune system weakened. Large amount of oxygen have the power of destroying harmful infectious bacteria, while preserving the good ones.

Drinking pure, clean water is essential to all functions of the body, including keeping our brains and memories alert. Water purifies and protects our body from harm, inside and out. Giving thanks after a purifying shower or bath reminds us that water is a gift that should be cherished and never taken for granted. Water is a live energy and responds to our mood. If we hold water in our hands before we drink it and feel sincerely grateful for its magical properties, it will bring the rejuvenating energy of the Earth inside of us.

Water is intimately connected to the Earth. In certain locations it is more energetically charged. In the presence of a body of water, you may have a powerful energetic experience as you release unwanted emotions and feel recharged and happy.

Mineral lakes around the planet are unique healing waters if you are willing and ready for the process to take place. Besides enhancing relaxation and blood circulation, mineral waters are known to help with muscle pain, joint stiffness, arthritis, eczema and even nasal congestion.

Oceans have natural healing powers because of the thousands of negative ions they produce in the air when water collides on the shore. Despite the negative sounding name, negative ions actually have electrical charges that produce a positive effect on our bodies, while positive ions are detrimental. When negative ions enter our bloodstream, they produce biochemical reactions that increase levels of the mood chemical serotonin. Natural serotonin has been proven to make us feel light and happy and helps alleviate depression and stress.

Waterfalls produce the most negative ions, having a highly positive effect on people's health, physically as well as emotionally. When we sit by a waterfall and stay still long enough, we receive an incredible sense of inner peace and belonging as the water's refreshing mist gently touches us. Like the waterfall, we may feel strong and important, knowing that our optimum mission is making sure that this water keeps running. We feel like one of the Earth's workers, proud and dedicated to keep life moving forward, proudly nurturing a deep sense of purpose.

As human beings, we bring unnecessary challenges to ourselves when it comes to choosing food. In terms of nutrition, we need to go back to the basics. Eating should be a blessed time where we feed our body, the temple that is allowing our Earth experience. Our temple needs to be honored and respected or it will break apart. Food is to be eaten and chewed slowly and not shoveled down. It's essential to eat food that boosts our mood and gives us energy. After a meal, if we feel heaviness in the stomach, bloated, or if we burp quite a bit, there is an excess of food, or it is the wrong choice for the body. Through experimenting with different foods, allergy tests, and the help of a nutritionist, our metabolic system will slowly guide us in the right direction. If we respect what our body agrees with, eating will give us pleasure and healthy support.

If we wonder about the ideal weight, it is the one where our body is not deprived of the right food and nutrients. If we can run a block or more without being totally out of breath, then we're probably at a comfortable weight. It isn't so much the weight but how we feel inside the body that gives us a clue on a healthy weight. It means breathing easily and fully, feeling alert and energized, and able to walk, run, exercise or swim with ease. It means that all our organs are freely functioning together. Some people are not meant to be skinny because it wouldn't be

73

enough to support their particular system. Diet often means depriving, when in fact it should all be about balance. We should not deprive ourselves of nutrients or constantly feel hungry, nor should we eat until we feel stuffed and sleepy. When our eating habits get out of hand and we are facing obesity, it is time to take a realistic look at the reasons causing us to put our health and entire life in jeopardy.

There are many reasons for obesity. It might be past or present emotional distress that pushes us to eat in order to silence the pain. Imbalanced glands and organs not functioning properly might be the problem. Obesity can also be genetically passed on from parents to children, which might be karmic. Karma should and can be understood and overcome through energy work. The goal is to pinpoint the emotions that caused the need to put and keep on the extra weight for protection. Healing our suppressed emotions will allow the body to release and slim down as we recognize and clear up our fears, anger and pain. In retrospect, it's imperative to learn about our metabolism but also about what we emotionally carry sometimes from a young age on.

One essential part of our well-being, health and balance is without a doubt friendship. If we choose to stand alone afraid of being hurt or betrayed, never getting touched, never exchanging ideas and feelings with other people, we are depriving ourselves of the very meaning of our passage on the planet. Such lack of exchange brings an emotional gap that is detrimental to our health at every level. Protecting ourselves from pain doesn't mean being deprived from such a human fundamental need.

Crystals are often used as healing enhancers. Crystals are empowered and highly charged with energy while in the earth. When removed from the earth, their charge depletes with time. If we believe in the healing power of crystals, the intention of using them as a tool of healing will restore the original crystal's energy. It becomes more powerful to us if we choose it because it agrees with our vibrations when we hold it. The crystal will charge even more through our connection to the Earth and to the Life Source along with our genuine healing intentions.

Colors consist of energy and vibrations so they have a strong influence in our life. Colors have healing energies, so we should pay attention to colors we surround ourselves for our clothing, car, home décor, etc. Colors and their shades are a reflection of our deepest emotions. If they reflect sadness or fear, such as grays and deep blues, or black, it would be helpful to slowly move toward happy supportive colors. Bright and energetic colors such as oranges, greens and pinks show and sustain a happy and hopeful state of mind.

Perfect physical health could be described as organs, cells and glands holding hands together and working in perfect harmony. It will take place when we pay attention to our body's signals. Is our body deficient in certain foods and vitamins? Or are we emotionally suppressing fear, pain and anger while ignoring and denying their importance? Our body is our soul's carrier. Would we allow the parts of our necessary car to break and not fix them before the car stops all together? Every discomfort, symptom and ache happening in the human body is there first and foremost to bring our attention to something going wrong. With time, lack of attention to the mechanism of our body will bring dis-ease and illness. We must pay attention and make changes or adjustments to our lifestyle before issues literally grow out of control.

The largest disease of this century, which we call cancer, is an emotional dis-ease of the heart. Our body has been created in perfect harmony and can heal itself if it remains loved and balanced. It is understood that we come to Earth wanting to feel emotions but are eventually consumed by them. The process of understanding and processing emotions is at times so lengthy and painful that it physically materializes as an illness before we decide to confront and fix what emotionally destroys us.

Some of us choose either prescription or recreational drugs or alcohol to fix or numb our emotional pain, which works by keeping the mind and the body anesthetized. A mind that is put to sleep is missing the will needed to heal itself. So as we can't seem to escape the pain, we give up. We ultimately find an illness to escape life, thinking that we will be done with our troubles. The first step to cure anything is to find its emotional source. If 70% of our energy is focused on emotional healing, the body would get rid of cancer and other diseases. Stagnant, negative emotions found inside our mind, body and soul are where the cancer cells make their nest.

Cancer cells will often be born in the part of the body where the sick emotions are withheld. As an example, a woman whose experience may include a divorce, abuse or betrayal might develop breast cancer as it is located close to the heart. A person feeling trapped where emotions and words are suppressed as if they can't breathe could develop lung cancer. If one doesn't speak their truth or speaks negatively, it might turn into throat, mouth or thyroid cancer. Holding onto resentment about something might cause colon cancer since negative emotions are held back like constipation. When we refuse to take a look within and work at releasing the debilitating emotions, cancer might spread, as everything is interconnected. When medical doctors decide to trust and work in collaboration with various therapists, including medical intuitive individuals to find where the emotions are suppressed, patients will respond quickly to treatment and the cancer is less likely to return.

Each unimaginable plague that confronts the world is a wake-up call for us to get back into balance. Unfortunately, we quickly move away from the reality check mode and forget, so one disease is replaced with another devastating illness.

The twenty-first century has seen yet another ravaging and life-changing calamity, the Corona virus. It takes a common enemy for the human race to pay attention, an enemy that we can't see and can't put down. It is calling for a global awakening that we have yet to acknowledge. The change must begin within us even if we can't conceive that one person's happiness can ripple and touch thousands of lives. It is our duty to seek balance and therefore happiness which will make the world a better place for all. There should be no room for selfishness, greediness, anger and vengeance. Mother Earth is also rebelling against the enormous abuse done to her and we are reaping what we sow.

Our souls are magnificent because of being part of the Life Source, but once in the human circle of emotions, we have to be hit hard to get things right.

According to the Google dictionary, the meaning of balance is "a condition in which different elements are equal or in the correct proportions." Our body is equally composed of four parts which are the *physical, mental, emotional and spiritual*, whether we acknowledge their existence or not. We need those four components to be addressed equally, meaning that each body needs attention for us to become and remain healthy.

We have talked about the physical and emotional bodies, but mental health is an essential factor to our equilibrium. It is represented by our thoughts and attitudes, as well as how we value our worth in the world. Mental illness and imbalance has multiple possible roots. It could be brought as a residual, karmic element that is not totally integrated but which could be spiritually, energetically resolved in time. In other instances, the soul reincarnates with a disturbed mind, remaining that way in order to rise above rejection and hardship while living in a harsh world that focuses on perfection. It can also bring soul-awakening to the parents helping them develop unconditional love and acceptance. If during pregnancy a soul does not feel welcome due to an unhealthy parental situation or it has a change of heart realizing that the chosen life has too many sacrifices to be endured, this could result in the child refusing to acknowledge and respond to the outside world. There are infinite physical and spiritual reasons for mental issues.

Schizophrenia is often diagnosed among people who are aware of the spirit world. From an early age, some schizophrenia patients hear, see or feel spirits, which frightens them as they don't know how to express or control what they are experiencing. Western medicine might conclude that they are mentally disturbed without considering the spiritual point of view. Therefore, some highly intuitive people may find themselves literally going crazy. If the problem is addressed early in time, spiritual support may help the person come to term with their psychic gift.

Several physical theories of health reasons are believed to be responsible for Alzheimer's disease and/or dementia. Those terrible diseases affect an individual's thought process and memory. This is why, from a spiritual aspect, a soul will often shy away from their past memories of pain, shame or regrets haunting their present reality, into a world of their own called Alzheimer or Dementia. It is not a conscious choice but most likely a comfortable progressive way to slip into a safer place.

Some mental illnesses can be healed or resolved but not all of them because this is the experience the soul signed up for.

As we understand, curing means relieving symptoms of a disease and becoming sound and healthy again. It would be beneficial for people to be cured and healed using a combination of medicine and energy healing practices. The first phase of healing could be self-exploratory. Prior to going to a physician and filling up pages of questions about our medical history and physical condition, we should make time to assess our emotional state. It might begin with reflecting from childhood to the present to seek where our feelings have been suppressed. This process would jumpstart our healing path in conjunction with western or holistic medicine, if an illness has already manifested in our body. If we decide to live in fear or denial of any suppressed emotional wounds, it will grow out of proportion like a weed in our minds. We must voluntarily weed things from within, and live freely.

LOVE FREELY LIVE FULLY

Living a long life is possible if the soul contract allows it. We have the capability to heal and rejuvenate our body. In order to accomplish this, we have to aim for balance and harmony with ourselves and others, which is challenging with the accelerated pace of modern times on Earth. Our higher self which remains in the Life Source is emotionless and totally at peace with all there is. The multiple dramas that we create on Earth in order to experience emotions do not exist out of the physical body. So as to achieve a healthy longevity, we should aim for inner peace and serenity as much as possible. Once again, meditation, yoga and other practices are helpful to temper the stress of everyday life. The energy of the people whom we choose to surround ourselves with has a strong influence as well on what produces peace or stress within us. However, becoming a hermit and remaining in a bubble would be counter-productive to experiencing the Earth as intended. Finding balance is about not to allow the outside world to invade and throw off our inner space.

Taking care of our spiritual body means that we stay connected and supported by the Life Source through the highs and lows of our life journey. Many of us, no matter which belief system or religion we embrace, talk to God or the Life Source or to other high beings. This communication when coming from a deep and genuine soul raises our vibrations because it connects us to a higher consciousness where there is no ego. The energy of this prayer coming from a loving intention goes into the Life Source, is heard, and answered. When we pray for our loved ones, the prayer doesn't apply only to them, but joins all the other prayers supporting humanity and the planet because it comes from unselfishness, compassion, and unconditional love.

There are no ideal words or recipe for prayers. The Life Source and the universe respond strongly and irrefutably to positive requests. It means giving thanks and showing gratitude for what we have and what else we wish for, as if it has already happened. When we stand in a state of knowing that everything is possible, without doubts using trust and strong faith, is when our desire becomes reality. We attract into our life what we absolutely believe to be possible. Feeling deep within our mind, body and soul the joy of having our needs fulfilled and being truly appreciative for having our wish come true works miracles. We may say, "Thank you for my perfect health" if that is what you wished for or "for my ideal job" or "for my ideal solution," visualizing the issue as already resolved. Even if we don't see how our desire will be granted, we need to keep the faith. Once we believe it without a doubt, it will materialize if it is for our highest good. Two things need to be understood. Hoping for a miracle without participating in any necessary process of making the wish come to fruition may not result in fulfillment of our expectations. Secondly, praying for someone else to be relieved of their ailment without knowing why they brought it on themselves, whether they want to be cured or they are willing to do the steps necessary for healing might bring us frustration and disappointment. Still, prayers for others are always a gift worth giving.

In retrospect, when people ask why we look so healthy and happy, we should share this simple recipe: "I make sure that my body resonates with the food I eat instead of dieting, and I work at being in balance. I make time to just be and connect with the Earth and the Life Source. I regularly work at clearing my toxic emotions. I make a point of focusing and being grateful about what is good within me and in my environment because all is energy and what I focus on grows and expands. I am seeking joy no matter where I am in my life because without joy and faith, no matter what I acquire, something will always be missing."

Society is in profound distress because we are desperate and giving our power away to quick fixes. Now is a good time to take a different direction.

The ideal way to change the world is to first and foremost take care of ourselves. The only way to reach peace on Earth is for each of us to achieve and nurture peace within ourselves. We must make sure to heal damaging emotions and actively seek a healthy balance. Loving freely beginning with ourselves and living fully showing the path to others is the dawn of a miracle cure.

7

AKASHIC RECORDS or BOOK OF LIFE

With so many earthly catastrophes and hardships happening all over the planet, we wonder what in the world is happening? In fact, the question should be, "what is happening in my world"? What many of us can't figure out is what we are meant to be and to do. Are we special in any way, we often wonder? Do we have any kind of purpose in life that makes the challenges meaningful and worth going through? The answer is YES to all of it. The fact is, that we create our own reality. We do it all ourselves, every minute of every day.

The process through which we create our reality is simple. Every single thought, every wish and desire, every fear and doubt, as well as every loving or selfish intention, everything that our mind produces, gets automatically printed in the universal computer. Ultimately, it builds a compilation of possibilities from which we create our reality. The universal computer bears many names; it's called the Book of Life or the Hall of Records but is best known as the Akashic Records.

Akashic is an ancient Sanskrit word relating to space or ether. This space, like a giant library, gets constantly encoded with records, memories, and the history of human experience. The Akashic Records are made of vibrations acting as magnets. When we have thoughts, either joyful or fearful, any thoughts, words, deeds, productive or destructive intents and feelings, anything that's created in the mind, is magnetized and attracted by the Akashic vibration surrounding all there is.

We can't escape this. It's almost like a diary where we write absolutely everything. So we have to remember that the universe has access to this particular diary. If we're afraid of something happening, the universe reads it but only picks up and acts on key words, like accident, for example. If we hold the fear of having an accident, the universe will bring it forward in our reality, as it's what we keep on our mind. Therefore holding positive thoughts becomes an essential part of happiness. We must embrace the thought of being safe instead of fearing the worst outcome, of being healthy instead of the fear of sickness, and of being financially comfortable instead of anticipating being broke.

The Book of Life's purpose is to keep the memory of our history so nothing is forgotten. It allows us to knowingly evolve. If we were to forget our past entirely and begin life today, we would have no background to move forward from, oblivious of the meaning of our existence. So the records are precious and thoroughly kept in order for us to better understand our whereabouts from life to life. Akashic records contain the entire history of every soul since the beginning of creation. It's a tool used to better grasp the dynamics of our present life. It helps explain our choices and passion for one career or another. Life histories also shows why a young child is a music or mathematics prodigy. We might have unexplainable fears of dogs, cats, heights, drowning, car accidents, flying, etc., without any way of getting over them. By accessing our records, our past history will give us the cause and allow us to release the fear through knowingness and energy work.

Akashic Records are accessible for us to validate what we intuitively feel deep down. However, the records should be read and used with the sole intention of supporting how we have already decided to go about our life purpose. It would be detrimental to the soul's evolution to seek the most advantageous and least challenging ways to achieve our goals. The records are not meant to be consulted for us to find our purpose without efforts or having to overcome rough patches. The human experience is about finding within ourselves what we are made of, what our intuition, passion and soul is desperately longing for, one step at a time. Going to the records will show us why we are attracted so strongly to a particular ambition and give us confirmation. Developing passion for life and its secrets is the perfect antidote to an opportunistic attitude. The records are meant to be a support system on our journey of self-discovery.

Seeking the Akashic Records should take place after experiencing and practicing other forms of spiritual practice and growth, otherwise the information could be very confusing. For example, if we discovered that we committed murder in a past life, would we be able to comprehend the ramifications, the karma and needs of our soul this time around? What if we were royalty or wealthy in a previous life and poor today? We might feel victimized by life and society, thinking that life is unfair and that others owe us. Or would we understand that not being compassionate and generous in the past life brought us to experience poverty and develop those virtues now? Depending on our level of spiritual awareness, too much information might not be processed properly or put to good use.

Being shown visions of the past or even future through the practice of meditation would most likely suggest to us that we are ready to handle more knowledge. Being prepared with the right attitude and intentions about what we will discover is essential to a positive outcome. It would be unwise to consult our records without such groundwork.

There are different ways to access our Akashic Records. There will be teachers and guides along the way to help us as long as the decision has been made to fulfill our life contract, of our own free will. There are also intuitive and clairvoyant people who can assist us in reading our information. Nevertheless, the most important requirement is to have an honest, genuine intention in order to honor our life's mission and destiny. Then, all the doors will open for us.

The Akashic Records contain our entire history, even lives pertaining to experiences on other planets. This particular information is not necessarily accessible to all human beings. Our level of awareness needs to be ready to accept and wrap our minds around the idea of other forms of life before being able to retrieve and comprehend this part of our evolution.

Without a doubt, we create our lives with each thought that we allow and nurture in our mind and nest in our heart. It's a choice. Like in our daily diary, we should become mindful of what we think and say repeatedly knowing that the Akashic Records will send all of it back to us, no matter what it is. If in the silence of our mind without even speaking words, we are judging, resenting, or putting someone down, any of those thoughts, as soon as we give birth to them, are printed and returned to us like a boomerang. Therefore, we must keep in mind what we wish to receive. The universe is there to support us in any direction we decide to go. As we wish for vengeance on someone, it will ripple back to us. If we spread love, compassion and joy around, without a doubt we will reap that one way or another. If we catch ourselves making a judgment about someone or any unhealthy thoughts or feeling that we would not appreciate to receive, we can cancel and change it into a sincere, loving, compassionate thought or comment.

In the human body, we are in training. Anger, resentment, fear, jealousy, envy and more will come to mind. It doesn't have to live there and take residence. We should cancel those thoughts and retrain ourselves until our thoughts make us feel good and proud. Our feelings divulge to us if our thoughts are constructive of wellness and happiness.

8

SUICIDE

Suicide, or the act of terminating our own physical life, is the ultimate act of last resort, attempting to defeat an invisible enemy called 'pain'. What throws us over the edge is usually related to the inner child's wound which we suppressed and hid deep in our soul. The emotional agony will either materialize into physical illness or into an unbelievable mental and emotional abyss. We will then either reach for help and find the courage to release and heal the trauma or give up on life altogether.

Is it a crime, a sin, or a punishable transgression for us to take our own life? It is a misconception to believe that the death of the physical body is the end of the emotional torment. Once the soul exits the body, it remains in the same state of despair and is oftentimes haunted by strong guilt and regrets. The soul usually finds itself more depressed then ever. It remains in a dark state, feeling hopeless and unworthy of reuniting with the higher self within the Life Source. Once out of the human flesh, no matter how we died, our soul is called to enter a magnificent light filled with unconditional love leading back to the Life Source. At that moment, our soul realizes that aborting its human experience because it felt overwhelming was pretty much an act of cowardice. We came to Earth with a mission for a journey made of experiences to help us grow. We chose and signed a contract with our own agenda and free will. Committing suicide is deciding to give up on our purpose and commitment. Sadly, our soul might wander for a long time feeling lost, confused and unworthy.

Have we ever considered the importance of a single day of our life? Have we experienced days where things took an unexpected turn for the better?

What looked like things totally falling apart one day, feeling like our world was crashing, suddenly, by some kind of heavenly intervention, was the beginning of an amazing new chapter. Would we give up, without a second thought, one day of our life? Would we give it away not knowing what this one day was intended to be? What if it is the day we would reconnect with a long lost love? Is it the day we are offered our dream job? Is it the day we found that our illness can be cured? Is it the day we wake up with a deep rooted sense of purpose that we couldn't comprehend before? Is it the day that the love we always imagined crosses our path and finds us? The list is infinite as to what can happen tomorrow that would change our world and bring us a joy never imagined. Should we give up the day before it all happens?

Suicide, no matter the cause, will always create consequences and karma to be addressed on the next incarnation. The same challenges will most likely increase the next life around through the soul's free will. There's no such thing as punishment from God or the Life Source. Our Life Source only asks us to stay connected to our higher self so that we don't go through the whole experience of life alone, feeling helpless.

From the human perspective, some situations feel like a dead end, so physically or emotionally unbearable or unfair that suicide seems the only way out. When hopelessness brings us to purposely end our physical life, and the Light Source comes for us to cross over, we might realize that we have made a mistake by giving up on our life contract while hurting our family and friends. On the other hand, once out of the body, if our soul believes deep down that suicide was not about running away, giving up on a life's mission that is not living up to our expectations, or fleeing from fear or responsibilities, then the soul should go back home to the Life Source happily and free of shame or regrets. It will always be self-judgment. Still, the evolution expected from this particular lifetime will have to be addressed again until achieved.

SUICIDE

Losing a loved one leaves a devastating gap within us, but losing someone through suicide, turns our world upside down and drags us into an infinite distress sometimes coupled with unshakable feelings of guilt. We wonder what would have happened if I had paid more attention to the signs, I helped or intervened more, I taken him or her to therapy or I never left the person alone? The process of grieving will take us from disbelief to pain and anger. Then we question the unfairness of the loss, accusing God or the Life Source for taking or not protecting our loved one. Anger and resentment will keep the departed soul sad and tormented even more. It is only adding to their guilt because they feel responsible for our pain. Achieving forgiveness is the only way to liberate both of our souls from everlasting pain. Each of us has free will and we are solely in charge of our destiny. Torturing ourselves thinking that we could have stopped someone's suicide is futile. It cannot be stopped; if the person has firmly reached that decision, they will find a way.

All of this raises the question, how can we prevent suicide? There is no magic spell; there is only being present and attentive to a person's behavior, especially while they show signs of depression aggravated by self-imposed solitude. It might be a mistake to disregard the symptoms, hoping that they will pass with time. As soon as we realize a behavior that is increasingly dispirited, it would be wise to help them reach out for help. Consulting with a medical counselor and with an intuitive who would be able to tap into present and past life issues quickly to see where the problem lies. Ultimately it could be addressed and hopefully healed.

People of all ages, especially children and young adults, would benefit from being exposed to the spiritual side of life, learning that they are not alone but always guided by God or the Life Source that created them. It should be highlighted that no matter what belief system we embrace, every action we take brings consequences meaning creates karma. From childhood to adulthood, most of us don't realize how valuable life is and wondering what is expected from us. Without such understanding, we are ready to quit when things get tough. We all need to know why we were born. We need to actively seek our life's purpose in order to make conscious choices. Before going through hard times, we must be taught ways of dealing with emotions and situations other than taking our own life to stop our suffering.

As parents, spouses or close friends, we are not impartial therapists or healers being emotionally involved and sometimes, being oblivious of the part we play in the problem. To be honest, there is also the reality that most of us have not yet addressed and healed our own emotional wounds. When we feel that someone we care about is showing suicidal signs, it is wise to intervene by reaching out for a professional support system, both through standard western medicine and holistic healing medicine, including intuitive counseling.

LOVE FREELY LIVE FULLY

Following a suicide, in time, a conversation with the departed through a medium might bring answers that help our healing to take place.

After suicide, once souls find themselves out of the body, our sincere prayers will lighten the burden of their souls helping them to connect with the Life Source. It is also important to be empathetic to those who suffer terrible losses through suicide, offering unconditional love and support while allowing them the time and space to grieve.

It is of the utmost importance to remember that we were created by a Life Source no matter what religious or spiritual beliefs we acknowledge. We are never alone but always guided by the Life Source through our higher self. Let us be open to receive a much loving and powerful guidance for a smoother Earth ride.

9

DEATH, CROSSINGOVER, LIFE REVIEW, SOUL FAMILY

Death by definition is the end of the terrestrial experience for a human body. On a spiritual level, it can also represent a lifeless soul. The Life Source that created the whole universe is energetically feeding and supporting us, keeping everyone and everything alive physically, mentally, emotionally and spiritually. When we choose to ignore our connection to the Life Source and to our fellow human beings, we become depleted of our life vitality and begin to die. The entire universe is made of energy surviving through its restless interaction, and the reason why we must stay connected.

We must participate in the circle of life one way or another. We need to help each other using our individual talents and gifts, embracing a cause we are attuned with such as saving the planet or participating in anything that will support the balance of every living creature. If we choose to isolate ourselves, falsely believing that we can survive mostly on our own, we would begin dying off like a TV set disconnected from the outlet. We would no longer be fueled with the life energy and would begin fading away emotionally, mentally and spiritually and finally, physically. We would still be physically alive, but there would no longer be any joy, spark or fire within.

When our life contract is coming to an end, our physical vehicle will no longer sustain life because it will be time to go home. Our soul orchestrates its entire journey ahead of time before being reincarnated. It chooses the karma and experiences to be addressed according to the level of evolution we wish and aim to attain. But sometimes, we decide to go before our contract is fulfilled because we are overwhelmed and no longer up to the task. We might also feel victimized by life, feeling bored or unappreciated. We may not understand that our sole responsibility is to remember our purpose which we willingly chose and accepted. If we go on, not realizing that evolution is achieved by stepping over roadblocks and taking in the lessons, we may subconsciously create an accident in order to step out of a life that we don't appreciate. Our body can also generate a disease in order to escape the challenges of our current life, instead of facing the obstacles and growing stronger from them. Leaving ahead of time is a choice which will bring the consequences of having to do it all over again to conclude the soul contract made with itself.

If we are exiting the planet through a disease, there will be soul family members from the Life Source visiting us in the room from days to a few weeks prior to the time of passing. They will come to support and prepare us for the shift so we are peacefully looking forward to finally go home, mostly exhausted of sustaining pain. When our life contract comes to an end, we have no more interest in the physical realm for food, conversation, television or anything else, which means that we are disconnecting with anything earthbound. Subconsciously we start telling our body to shut off because we are ready to go. It is a process. The body will slowly begin shutting down. The last breath is a wonderful relief for the soul which immediately escapes out of the heaviness of the flesh. The physical death of the body feels like falling asleep on a plane and waking up at destination, not remembering anything in between. Upon our awakening, a bright light is opening up with excited people waiting for us inside the light; the spirit world is welcoming back the soul joining its soul family. Right away, our soul sees everyone and everything as pure energy, as if it had been looking through a very heavy curtain that has just been lifted. There are no more obstacles and everything happens instantly. Our soul hears angels singing and when angels move, it sounds almost like the wind brushing the leaves of a tree. Our soul has to be in complete acceptance to move forward, with no fear, as we all have free will. After another experience in physical form for its evolution, our soul returns home. It is that simple, dying is just another transition, another birth. Everything has to come to an end in order for something else to begin.

If we exit life through an accident or any other sudden manner, there will be a soul family member, an angel or guide coming right away to help us feel safe while crossing over, making the transition from the extremely heavy gravity of the planet Earth into the light leading back to the Life Source energy.

A soul family is made of the group of spiritual beings to whom we belong, and with whom we evolve and learn in the spirit world between incarnations. A soul family varies from hundreds to thousands of souls or more. Under certain circumstances, two groups could merge; for example, in an Earth catastrophe that would take many lives at once, those souls would cross over and join the same group because they bonded within similar experiences. As we enjoy our Earth family here, we also often reincarnate with the same soul mates intending to work on karma created in previous lifetimes. Soul mates will change and occupy different roles in each other's lives in order to support the learning process on Earth.

Free will always prevails and it is possible for a soul to refuse the invitation to go back home after leaving the body, when the Light Source opens the way. Many reasons may cause our soul to stay behind instead of crossing over right away. It could be confusion due to our belief system or religion. If we believe that because we didn't respect or follow rituals and rules, and there will be repercussions, we might refuse to go. It could be that our soul sees its Earth family's despair and decide to remain. Some souls are very attached to the physical realm; they might have never given a second thought to spirituality and

110

decide to stay in the physical world. Once we encounter the purest and most unconditional essence of love as the Life Source opens up the light for us, we might not feel good enough and worthy to cross over. The love is so absolute that we might not feel deserving to accept the embrace. It might be astonishing to realize the immensity of the Life Source total acceptance and joy about us coming home. There are no terrestrial words or comparisons to describe the awe of that moment. When the Life Source comes, if we decide to stay earthbound, the light will wait for a while then disappear. It will honor the soul's free will to stay.

The soul always has the choice to reconsider its choice and the Light Source would once again open up a tunnel of light and show us the way. The Light Source is always welcoming us home if we so desire. If we never believed in God or any higher power, for example, chances are that we won't even ask for the Life Source to reopen the light passage. The belief system of the present incarnation will create our soul's reality. It's all about what our soul believes it deserves. As the Life Source comes to welcome us back home where we belong, even if our soul feels ashamed of its mistakes, it is still invited in the light with open arms to review our life and our purpose. Once our life review is done, if our shame, guilt or even anger against ourselves or life is overwhelming, our soul might progressively process it all, or could go on punishing itself. The soul might think that it is not worth being loved or given a chance to redeem itself. It might then enter into a self-isolation dark space, refusing the Life Source's help for clarity. It's what we might consider Hell as the soul feels the loving light calling but considers itself undeserving of accepting it.

This self-punishment is not an eternal condemnation. The spiritual soul family, guides and angels are keeping abreast of the soul's progress. And, we can rest assured that family's and friend's prayers are powerful tools to remove fear and induce our loved one's soul to seek the Life Source light which will then return for it. Once our soul crosses over willingly, it will be allowed to travel back and forth wherever it's needed to visit, guide, and watch over the loved ones left behind. They are with us as soon as we think of them because the notion of time and space applies to planet Earth and not to the spirit world. In fact, the past, present and future all happen simultaneously even if it's a difficult concept for the human mind to grasp.

Once our soul gets out of the body, floats a little and enters into the light with our loved ones, we feel welcome, cherished, and safe. Flashes of images amazingly reveal to us all the important events that took place in our life. Among other things, the soul's life review outlines every instance in which we helped someone else, how it made people feel and the domino effect that kindness had on countless of others. For every opportunity we had and didn't show compassion, give forgiveness or missed a chance to offer support, our soul will feel the pain, sadness or consequences caused by our behavior. Our soul will then judge or evaluate its degree of life success or failure. It's up to our soul to forgive its mistakes and weaknesses or condemn its fallacy. If we didn't recognize our wrongdoing during the physical life, after leaving the body, the vibration of our self-judgment might very well attract our soul to a low, dark, energy plane. If our soul can't acknowledge its wickedness and still seeks power, it would not be able to enter the light because it doesn't vibrate at the same frequency. A soul cannot enter a space that it has nothing in common with. Therefore the soul would stay in the earthbound plane because it's still longing for the illusion of control on the physical realm. With time, that soul might come to realize its predicament, seek help and move forward.

There are two instances when our soul goes through a spiritual experience while still very much connected to the physical body. One is when we enter into a coma whether it is induced or not; the soul being on some kind of time off or attunement. Once our soul gets back inside our body, we will not remember what went on during the time off period no matter how long it lasted. Our soul may need orientation because it might not be quite fully equipped for what is coming in our future or not successfully following its life's purpose, needing help on the spiritual or emotional level. Instead of choosing physical death, our soul might be travelling back and forth for a period of time to be educated and attuned so it can continue the journey as planned. On the other hand, our body might be so damaged by a disease or an accident that we might choose to give up our present incarnation. It could have to do with multiple, debilitating physical issues and a lot of pain, or we might not want to impose the ordeal on our family. Our soul might just realize that it has lost track of its purpose and decide to try to do better during the next passage on Earth.

What we call near death experience or NDE offers us a glance of the spirit world. Our soul's intention is not to shut off the body in order to die; on the contrary, the soul is seeking a wake-up call! Near death experiences mostly happen to us when we seem to have lost our way. Being allowed to glimpse the other side reminds us where we came from, see the light, and perhaps cross over long enough to gather the meaning and purpose of our present incarnation. The aftermath of a NDE may not be pleasant depending on the severity of what caused the dying experience. Again, our soul always chooses the outcome.

We've all heard people say, "No one ever came back from the dead to tell us what it's like on the other side." Actually, loved ones who have passed on communicate with us in many ways all the time, from flickering lights to making objects fall or disappear and find their way back again. We might think of a loved one and out of the blue a meaningful song plays on the radio or you view a car's license plate that means something special and familiar. Our loved ones often come back in our dreams, giving messages. At times, when we are awake or dozing off, they might caress us on the cheek or touch our hair. It may happen that a flowery perfume comes from nowhere and makes us smile, or a pipe's sweet odor in the air might remind us of our beloved grandfather. Once we lose someone, the intensity of the emptiness in our heart often makes us oblivious to any such signs but rest assured that from the spirit world they are eager to communicate how they feel and offer guidance to their family and friends.

Death means simultaneously ending one experience and being reborn in another. It means joining our soul family and making plans for the next experience. Energy is eternal and we simply keep transitioning from one form of life to another for our soul to evolve at every level possible.

LOVE FREELY LIVE FULLY

10

PETS, THEIR PURPOSE AND REINCARNATION

Animals are beings that are, at all times, connected to their essence of love and to the Life Source. They are, contrary to our belief system, highly evolved beings who have, for the most part, mastered emotions and power struggles and are ready to serve a meaningful purpose. Those souls are willing to incarnate in an animal body with total awareness of their mission and equipped with unconditional love, compassion and strong forgiveness abilities. Nonetheless, they take on an Earthly body which includes its own personality traits.

Still, animals may have to go through some karma or life teachings based on past life behavior. If a dog bites someone, for example, was it to defend itself or a loved one? Was it because this pet was trained to attack instead of being loved? Was the animal just frustrated because it doesn't like his collar, his food or kids who hurt or bother him? If the dog has a bad temper, built up anger and he bites, then he does create karma, which is based on the intention before taking action. All God's creatures have free will.

Animals bring humans happiness because their essence is pure and their love without conditions. Holding a fragile newborn animal wakes up an emotion through our entire body where we feel in awe, as if nothing in the world could alter that moment. We have so much to learn from animals, like living in the moment. For instance, our pet is ecstatic to see us return home every day no matter how long they waited. Our pets do not build up anger or resentment, get upset or withhold affection.

Pets that are particularly precious to us are in fact soul mates, being part of our soul family. Therefore, many of us feel that we get along better with our pets than with people. Besides giving devoted love and affection, our pets do not betray, lie or ask for us to change and compromise. It seems ideal compared to the tribulations that some relationships bring forth in our lives, but then again, we were born as humans in order to evolve and grow in wisdom among our fellow men. As much as we sometimes prefer the company of our four-legged companions, they are not a replacement for human relationships. Furthermore, they might turn out to be our excuse to stay away from commitment and growth. If our pet has been taking the emotional and physical place of a mate for a long time, it would be healthy for the pet/owner relationship to be re-evaluated. Why did we replace a friend or a mate with a pet for so long? The question should be addressed for our own sake and for our animal companion.

If our pet's soul needed to be born as a human being, it would have been. Animals choose to be so because they are in a higher realm of reality, living in the moment instead of dwelling on the past or figuring out an ideal outcome. Of course, being in the flesh, they still enjoy food, play time, love and may create karma. Most of all, they do the work they wholeheartedly signed up for; filtering, processing and lighting up our emotional and physical issues for us to maintain balance and live fully. Animals live at such high frequencies that the physical body can only sustain life for a short period of time within each incarnation.

It would be wise to honor our favorite animal's life choice and let it be a pet, training and allowing them to sleep on their own bed, eating their own food. If our dog insists on sleeping on our bed, chances are that we created this need for our own benefit. It might be favorable to reinstate proper roles and for both of us to learn boundaries and limitations. When our pet can freely fulfill its purpose, we might do the same and regain trust in our peers to sustain our evolution through experiencing human love, compassion, and forgiveness.

On the other hand, we should pay more attention to our pet's behavior because they teach us so much about our own personality traits. If we were born in perfect harmony within ourselves, the animal that would come to us would be in perfect harmony as well. As always, we attract who we are, mirroring each other in order to heal and grow. Our energy emanates a certain level of self-acceptance and self-confidence; consequently, we will attract a pet that resonates to our frequency. We, as human beings, are not born in perfect balance having to learn through lessons and experiences. Thus, the way we come across our favorite animal often feels like a match made in heaven and indeed it is, most of the time. If we were an overactive child and a little wild, we can expect that our pet will probably reflect our personality. If we suffered from abandonment or rejection and we are much in need of tenderness, love and affection, we might find our pets first having trust issues as well as craving much attention.

LOVE FREELY LIVE FULLY

The reason a beloved friend made a commitment to us as a life companion is mostly to give us undivided love and emotional support on a segment of our journey. After a certain number of years, once we have integrated what we had to learn during that life chapter, our faithful friend is free to return to the Life Source. If the owner and animal souls are in agreement, and if it is what is needed for each other's highest good, our pets will come and go at different stages of our life to hold the space again, when the time is right for both of us. Those special beings might have contracts with other soul family members in the interim. The animals also go through their own karma and life challenges while in the physical world. They go through sickness, handicaps, abandonment, grieving and pain of losing their owners, being abused and at times saving human lives.

If we wonder why and how we choose certain species of animals over others as companions, it is often coming from our past lives, karma and contracts already made between us and our animal soul mate. Those specific pets find and choose us and not the other way around. It might be a dog, cat, lion, possum, elephant, a bird, etc. We might find them as lost new born or hurt in our backyard, on the street, in the forest, on a faraway trip and we will nurse them back to health. This is how and why, through free will, some wild animals choose to enter our lives and can be tamed.

At the same time, it often reflects the deepest part of our personality. We may bond with a gold fish because we are not quite open to the outside world, preferring to look at what is going on out there and not necessarily participate in the world rat race. There would be a glass between us and the pet. We would take care of the fish without having our space invaded. It would be interesting to wonder if we keep people at a safe distance as well. If we take the example of a bird that we love and care for, it could represent a part of us feeling trapped in a cage, even a gold one.

LOVE FREELY LIVE FULLY

Our pets are soul mates who volunteered to help us navigate our present passage on Earth. They are very much an expression of where we stand on our life's adventure at any point in time.

11

RELATIONSHIPS, SOUL MATES, TWIN FLAMES, SEXUALITY

Falling in love is what most of us spend a lifetime dreaming of, or are desperately going after without a map or an instruction book. Is finding love a pure coincidence? What is a coincidence, if not merely steps forward from where we are to where we belong? Life, the universe and the Life Source will always bring us where we need to be for the next growth experience. As for falling in love, it happens when two people are both ready to undertake a huge transformation and a shift to embrace yet another part of their journey.

LOVE FREELY LIVE FULLY

Everything on the planet, including relationships, is a tool for humans to learn. Every human being is whole and complete but we are not aware of it. Relationships come in our lives to mirror to us what we don't see and acknowledge about ourselves. The main attraction on Earth for human beings is emotions; it's like Disneyland for souls. When we incarnate in the human flesh, we are quickly addicted to feeling a wide range of emotions. We crave experiencing the highs of love and sometimes the lows of pain and sadness. When two people experience sexual relations, it brings them to a deeper emotional part of their being; humans are longing for that connection. Our soul knows it all, but our body wants the experience. The closer we emotionally get to another, the deeper the intimacy. That is why we are eager to mate. Love is the miracle of life. It can't be bought or sold. It can't be forced or imposed. It just is.

Some of us find love early in our teenage years and spend a lifetime together with our mate. It is mostly because our souls know each other so well after having been together in multiple incarnations. We might return together knowing that we will need each other's support through hard times in our next challenging venture. It could also be that in past lives, we kept missing the opportunity to grow old together and decided to dedicate this lifetime to getting to know and enjoy each other.

Another life scenario might be that we will have a series of relationships. Each mate is a teacher to the partner. If lessons to be learned are not processed and understood, every relationship will be based on the same pattern until we change the old, unhealthy behavior. It is of the utmost importance, in between relationships, to achieve closure. It means to face the reality and come to terms with taking responsibility, releasing anger and resentment and offering forgiveness. Making time to regain our balance is also mandatory and only then, will we be ready for a new beginning.

LOVE FREELY LIVE FULLY

Another aspect of the love relationship dynamic is also based on where our soul began the present journey. That means addressing love karma encountered or created in previous lives which we have agreed to resolve this time around.

If we desire to be in a relationship but find ourselves alone for a long period of time, we may be in the fear mode. Proclaiming that we are ready for love is not the same as being ready. After having been emotionally hurt many times over in previous experiences, we need to come to terms with being skeptical and defensive about love. The obvious result of this fear will be to attract exactly what we are afraid of and unconsciously expecting. It's all about lessons and growth of the soul meaning how much karmic wisdom we have conquered, understood, and resolved. This will influence dramatically the quest for a long-lasting relationship.

Another pre-requisite to finding love is about learning to love and accept everything about who we are. Once we are in harmony with our own essence, it's natural to attract and recognize the same harmony within another. The essence of love is deeper and stronger than an emotion; it brings the entire body into lightness and joy. When we fall out of what we call love, it's because the love was conditional to begin with, like expecting the other person to make us happy and feel complete. It means that we are still looking outside of ourselves to fill up the empty space we feel inside. When our expectations are not met, the feeling of love fades away and we are left disillusioned and hurt. If we were connected to our essence, we would not look for another to complete us but for a person with whom to grow, to evolve further and to share our passion for life.

It might seem scary for us to invest in a long lasting relationship when we see couples growing apart and finally go their own ways after 10, 20 or 40 years. It often happens because one partner or both partners have stopped nurturing the union, taking it for granted instead of making mandatory time and space to kindle the relationship. When there is no more excitement or a sense of adventure, we forget that what we have is precious and priceless. When two people fall in love, they are somewhat at the same place in their evolution and they relate to each other. Time goes by and the mates evolve at a different pace and sometimes in different directions which can enrich each other's life or grow a wall. If one grows and evolves while the other stagnates, they might become strangers. Then they regard each other and don't like what they see. The one who doesn't invest in self-growth might feel shame, guilt, low self-esteem and even anger, feeling betrayed looking at a partner who is consciously and actively moving forward. The more evolved companion will see the other person as needy, feeling victimized by life, and carrying a negativity that's draining. So, people grow apart because they stop putting effort in themselves and in the relationship that stood as their loving support. At that point, a couple may part peacefully of their own accord or may leave with resentment and bitterness, subsequently creating karma.

RELATIONSHIPS, SOUL MATES, TWIN FLAMES, SEXUALITY

It's different when there are crimes committed against the soul. A crime against the soul is hurting a partner in a knowing way. It goes from cheating and lying to physical, verbal, or emotional abuse, it might be affected by substance addiction or by an undertow of unacknowledged anger never dealt with. When a partner is no longer honored and respected in such a manner, it's time to part, understanding that the dynamic is destructive and no longer based on love.

Afterwards, each person is responsible for grieving their loss, understanding the particulars of the break-up, achieving healing and seeking balance in their life once again.

If a crime was committed, the couple most likely will eventually return to Earth together, to learn respect and self-respect, forgiveness and understanding to finally part if necessary, this time without negative karma. The two souls might sign up together again, but this time in different roles or reincarnate apart to experience something else and grow. It all depends on their choices between lives and how karma and lessons were integrated in the last experience together. Imagine a play on Broadway lasting for weeks. When the play is over, these actors may choose a different role or a different play or not act for a while in order to regroup. Life is a play; when the play is over, the soul group/family still exists. In the Life Source, there are no enemies, only different levels and planes of evolution.

It's an honor and responsibility for two souls to contract, share and support one another during their Earth experience; that is why not honoring such a contract is called a crime. Any level of love is energy and once created will never be extinguished or die. The love that we have given and received gets printed in our energy field, cellular memory and our Akashic records. If there was no crime or if it was mended and forgiven, this energy will enhance our own energy for eternity. We shouldn't be afraid to love, as love is the only real wealth and purpose for existing there is.

The term souls' mates come from our soul family. It is mostly souls with whom we had previous

134

incarnations in different roles and capacities. We once again agreed to sign a contract of support through experiences that will make each other's souls evolve further. Once our soul is born into a body, it subconsciously longs for its lost friends, souls that live inside our memories. Soul mates may show up in our life as our own gender or as the opposite sex, as spouses, lovers or friends, long term co-workers or neighbors, as our children or parents or as our pets. They are a safe place for growth and learning tolerance, acceptance, patience and forgiveness among other virtues. We should seek to understand the life contract dynamic agreed upon and give each other permission to learn and to grow. It means that it can be fun, easy and rewarding to spend time together. It also means that we will mirror each other's flaws, fears and disappointments in order to grasp self-love, self-acceptance and forgiveness. This is the role of soul mates, which doesn't guarantee a relationship without road bumps. As soul mates, we don't belong to each other but we might belong with each other.

Most of the time, romantic soul mate recognition involves physical and spiritual chemistry which are both signs of past life connection and most likely of a significant relationship. There is much more insight needed in order to maintain a long-lasting commitment. Once we fall in love, we should make a point of finding constructive ways to move our relationship forward. It would be ideal to relentlessly talk together to share both our likes, dislikes, fears, dreams, goals and belief systems, which would help us to get to know each other at a deeper level. Instead, we often blindly wish that the partner will live up to our unknown expectations. To make things worse, most of us prefer to ignore what is annoying us, foolishly hoping that it will change with time. If either mate feels that sharing each other's deepest thoughts and outlook on life is a waste of time, we should wonder if it's worth going into this relationship. Multiple romantic soul mates may cross our path during our lifetime as planned before birth, and our free will determines the outcome. A particular life lesson may be learned from one or multiple soul mates, unless a contract is signed with a specific soul from a previous karma. Relationships are stepping stones toward our soul's expansion.

A stronger bond than soul mates exists, called twin souls or twin flames. They come from a soul or consciousness that split in two. Both part of the same consciousness or soul will incarnate in a different body and follow their own agenda in order to gather a larger amount of Earth experience. Their goal is to become more whole, balancing their female and male sides, ideally reaching a high level of wisdom and awareness. It has been that way since the beginning of time; from fish in the oceans, to animals and human beings, cells split in two reproducing and creating twin cells.

Twin souls are not only found in a romantic relationship or based on a sexual attraction; our twin soul may be a best friend. Everyone has a twin flame, an identical other soul with whom they are connected, but not necessarily incarnated with on the planet at the same time. The chance of meeting and staying in a long lasting partnership with our twin flame is based on how much each soul has evolved by dealing with karma and emotional baggage from present and past lives. Upon meeting, twin souls will be attracted like magnets and soon realize that they mirror each other in many ways. Twin souls don't automatically grow in the same environment, but they both have the same evolution to go through. It might come a time when they find each other unless one of them is not ready. The souls eventually are reunited in the Life Source.

A broad misconception is to think that finding our twin flame would be the ultimate and absolute relationship. It would be best to go on our journey, working on being the best version of us that we can be, physically, mentally, emotionally and spiritually. Life will bring forth what and whom we need for further learning and support. If we ever cross paths with our twin flame, and even if we recognize an instantaneous deep bond and a sensation of familiarity, feeling like we are home, we will soon realize that it is not a perfect and easy-going relationship. Although it is an ideal space for deeper healing, transformation and soul awakenings, all emotions, whether negative or positive, will be amplified between twin flames. If both souls are progressing at the same pace or level, they might meet when their awareness is developed enough for the relationship to bloom and enhance each other's progress and purging process. If one has accomplished a lot more growth than the other, it might create an unbearable gap, jeopardizing the relationship. Although extremely painful, souls would have to continue their healing journey and maybe try again later.

With relationship also comes sexuality, which is often the initial attraction. Souls either choose to be re-born within a male or female body in order to experience the different polarities, which in turn attract each other. The female and male energies inhabit in each body gender and are embraced at different levels of intensity and development.

When it comes to being amorous, a male energy is easily physically aroused by looking at an attractive partner. A female energy needs to feel physically and emotionally safe, respected and feeling desired. The female energy is tender and sensitive, which is attractive to the male energy although the feminine essence might be complicated to decipher. Then again there's more to intimacy than what joins two bodies together, multi characteristics level of chemistry is often the magical ingredient.

Genuine intimacy requires a definite amount of love and devotion. Many of us don't have our desires met at many levels within our romantic partnerships. Not talking the same emotional and physical language becomes a barrier when it comes to discussing our mutual likings. Sex, like everything else within a relationship, should be openly explored and talked about in a loving and non-judgmental fashion. Trust, self-esteem and physical issues should be discussed and addressed ahead of time. Hoping that our partner will miraculously heal fears and wounds from the past or guess what is right for us is not a realistic expectation. If because of ego, either of the partners doesn't welcome such conversation, it might indicate a lack of commitment toward the happiness of both people.

Sexuality within a true loving relationship is essential and healthy at many levels for the human body. When people are in the essence of love and experience a fulfilling sexuality, it creates a high vibration frequency balance and harmony that extends to every part of their bodies. It has an effect on veins, organs, glands and hormones as if everything was getting awaked and filled up with life force. When we ignore love and intimacy, everything inside us gets tensed and energy cannot flow freely. This is a precursor to physical illness. On an emotional level, fulfilling intimacy releases accumulated stress and worries cluttering our mind and positively improves our mood. Spiritually, it brings the partners into an altered state where they feel elated through their mutual connection to the Life Source.

On an etheric level, while making love with a true intimate partner, the female energy has many thoughts going through the mind such as wondering what the lover feels, smells, thinks about and wants. That's why a female's arousal takes a lot more time. During this period, multiple balls of colors are playing in the aura, according to her thoughts. The masculine energy has one aura ball mostly based on physical desire, and it grows larger and larger. Ultimately, the sexual tension gets high enough for the female energy to calm the thoughts and form one big aura which comes together with the male's energy aura. When the lovers are totally releasing all reservations, the vibrations of their combined auras reach out for the Life Source and achieve a state of bliss.

Intimacy is at the core of any loving sexual relationship. When two people's desire of connecting as one comes from deep down in their souls, it's almost like an out-of-the-body experience. The souls elevate and meet at a higher level which is what souls are longing for; this is the ecstasy. When partners cannot or choose not to perform a complete sexual intercourse, the intensity of the desire to reach a level of physical, emotional and spiritual closeness can be achieved by holding each other's bodies, kissing each other and caressing each other's body tenderly and meaningfully. Each partner must act with a genuine intention to please and wake up each other's sensuality and sense of well-being; in other words, making each other feeling alive. Intimacy means never to cease nurturing the person travelling through life with us. Nothing can be more sacred than opening ourselves up, mind, body and soul, to another human being; it should be acknowledged as such by both partners.

In this fast-paced time, where couples juggle demanding jobs and family, lack of time, energy or money and deal with fears and lack of self-confidence, dedication and a solid sense of priorities is required. We must remember that the foundation of our family, the fuel that keeps us up and running is the strength of our relationship. Before we allow everyone and everything to come first or be an excuse for postponing intimacy, it's crucial to plan and schedule time for keeping love and sexuality alive as a priority. This will consolidate the union and help reduce the stresses and the frustrations of everyday life. We have to find as many intimacies breaks as possible as long as both partners are honored, and once in a while, schedule a lengthy romantic evening. We shouldn't wait days before we sneak ten minutes of passionate kissing in the closet to keep the anticipation and excitement alive. As partners, we must work hand in hand at the responsibility of planning time.

The meaning of partnering is establishing a long-term win-win relationship based on mutual trust and teamwork, and on sharing of both risks and rewards.

MAKE YOUR LIFE
SPECTACULAR

We read great books, participate in illuminating seminars, watch, and listen to inspirational programs and get excited because here and there, we can relate to the teachings. And then what?

Now comes the free will part of the deal. What are we going to do with the knowledge that actually hit home this time?

Nothing has to be done or decided if the quality of your life is exactly where you want it to be. Put the book on the pile, keep going and be grateful!

However, if you need to reinvent your life keep this book at hand. Step back from the mountain of overwhelming necessary changes and make a detailed list of what needs to be done to get to your new comfort zone.

BEGIN the process one step at a time.

Keep in mind that strength comes from feeling gratitude for our existence. Happiness comes from feeling energized, all-around healthy, safely guided, and passionate for life's opportunities. Vibrant and clear channeled energy, high vibrations and steady balance are our ultimate goals to achieve a fulfilling Earth adventure.

Most of us go on with our busy, daily routine without paying much attention to balancing mind, body and soul. In the course of a day, we get bombarded from all sides with everyone else's drama, absorbing it on top of our own. We later wonder why we are physically exhausted, mentally overwhelmed, emotionally drained and spiritually disconnected. The lack of balance will eventually turn into confusion, lack of appetite and too much or no sleep. Periods of depression and stress will manifest into physical disease. Our body will get sick, our mind will fall into despair, and our soul will lose track of its path unless we make sure to acknowledge, honor and nurture the physical, mental, emotional and spiritual components of our being.

For our soul's evolution, we inhabit a physical vehicle for the purpose of experiencing the Earth challenges and resolving karma from previous lives. The body, in order to sustain our demands and operate at its full potential, has to be fed and kept running with appropriate food and exercise. Once we fully grasp that this body is a holy mode of transportation carrying our soul, we then make appropriate choices. In fact, it is never about being deprived of what we call good food and feeling victimized. It is always about using the highest vibration of nourishment, meaning food coming from Mother Earth, in order to sustain our healthy frequencies.

The Earth hands us many gifts to support perfect health and a precious one is water. Drinking pure water will ground and calm us down should we find ourselves on an emotional rollercoaster, instead of reaching out for food as a temporary salvation.

This precious liquid should be used as a cleansing tool in every way possible. When we bathe or shower, it should be with a grateful intention and blessings to this purifying agent. We should ask water to purify not only our body but our aura and our energy. Water will remove much toxicity we might have attracted unknowingly in office buildings, hospitals, heavy traffic jams, restaurants, airports, and other places. Highly sensitive people are empathic, meaning that we easily sponge or take on other people's energy. At times, it feels rejuvenating when we are around happy and healthy individuals. However, in our fast-paced world, some people's energy fields are infused with stress, emotional or physical pain, vibrating fears or simply mental fatigue. As empaths, at the end of the day, we might not realize that we are carrying someone else's luggage.

Being mentally depleted in addition to an overload of stress and responsibilities often creates an invisible emotional or mental 'dis-ease' that we might choose to ignore until we can no longer cope.

Our mental equilibrium has to be a priority if we wish to achieve balance and happiness. It means taking a step back and genuinely looking at where we stand on our chosen path. It implies using our free will and making decisions about where we are and what we want to achieve in our relationships and in our work life. It becomes a must to re-evaluate where we live and with whom we surround ourselves. It is about taking inventory of what we have accomplished so far, realizing what it will take to go the extra mile if a life makeover is needed to fulfill our purpose. Reaching out for help in order to get a better perspective or to get tools as support on the new path would be an inherent part of our decision to move forward.

Our mental condition is invariably intertwined with our emotional status. No matter how hard we suppress those troubling emotions and try to bury them in the deepest drawer we can find, they represent the best and the worse of us. Emotions are not meant to be banished or controlled; on the contrary, they serve as a barometer of what we feel. They are teaching us to pay attention. Our emotions are either a giant stop sign signaling to change direction and destination or a bright green light inviting us to safely push forward toward our next goal. Once again, it comes down to making a different choice once we realize we are off course.

The spiritual aspect of our human life is of the highest importance if we wish to navigate our Earth contract as easily as possible. As humans, it is imperative to be grounded to Mother Earth who nurtures our physical needs and also to stay connected to the Life Source who is dedicated to ease our sojourn in the physical world. Without such connections, we are spaced out, navigating without our necessary GPS. We are constantly feeling like we are running out of time. Only a few committed minutes a day is needed to tap into proper guidance and direction, thus managing our day more adequately.

To be grounded with Mother Earth means being as close to nature as possible. It also includes walking barefoot, standing or sitting on the grass or the beach to bond with the Earth. Dedicating a sanctuary or sacred space to ourselves in front of a window to be touched by the sun or the moonlight brings much needed comfort.

We could push it a step further and take long deep breaths through our nose which we exhale slowly through our mouth. With each breath we should feel our feet or body anchoring deeper into the ground, relaxing our shoulders, head and neck. While bathing in the light, for a few minutes, we should close our eyes, slow down the chit-chat of our mind, and just remain in the moment.

In that instant of stillness, we are practicing meditation, which is the art of clearing the mind and listening to guidance from the Life Source. Meditation is about listening and putting the on-going mental dialogue on pause. Meditation can also be achieved while taking a peaceful walk and bonding with nature sounds.

Making those few minutes a daily priority in our routine would recharge us in the morning and detoxify us from stress and unwanted energies at the end of the day. To be grounded to the Earth keeps us stronger instead of riding on an emotional rollercoaster. Having no separation from the Life Source allows our intuitive channel to be sharply attuned to guidance resulting in a better attitude toward our life events and more accurate decisions.

We have come this far in this book because we believe in something bigger then ourselves. We know that there's a Life Source who created all there is and who supports us through unconditional love here on Earth. Not only is it important to listen to its loving guidance, but asking or praying for what we desire is also an essential part of our spiritual balance.

Praying is about stating what we desire, which creates certitude in the universe about our intention and calls forward the realization. Giving permission to a power higher than ourselves to give us assistance is a must because the spirit world cannot trespass on our free will. Prayer is acknowledging that what we ask is already in motion, honoring who supports us, and believing that prayers are answered if genuine and for the highest good of all. Finally, we need to demonstrate gratitude by working jointly with the universe while avoiding a victim's point of view which is vital to a positive and blessed outcome.

As human beings we often behave as chess pieces on a board, simply being pushed every which way, without partaking in our physical, mental, emotional and spiritual wellbeing. In order to have a say about our path, we need to participate and be one with the universe, the Earth and the Life Source. It's critical to realize, that the course of our journeys are interconnected. The energy of everyone and everything is coexisting with us on the planet, near or far, echoes and impacts us. Therefore, it's vital to support other's growth as preciously as our own and to naturally love one another. Only then, will we be able to love freely and live fully.

The Life Source expects us to 'pay forward' anything that we are grateful for, no matter where we begin or what we can share, especially if we have conquered hard times and challenges; let's share what we finally comprehend.

EPILOGUE

We hear all kind of suggestions to reach a state of happiness, from meditation to affirmations. When, what and how is it supposed to show up in our lives? Is it an epiphany happening out of nowhere? How do we know that we are happy and that the feeling is there to stay?

Happiness and joy are made of our own recipe, one that we work on every day, a special blend that we progressively improve and ultimately share with others.

Here it is. We are avatars and a spark of our energy incarnate in a human body while our higher self stays bonded with the Life Source. As souls we have access to all knowledge but we still feel the need to experience everything first hand. We are students learning in books but having no idea about the real world applications when our life will be intertwined with others and flickering with emotions.

After each incarnation, we review the work we had signed for, what was accomplished, which lessons call for revision, and which karma we have brought to closure or which new ones we have created. Karma can be new challenges or amazing progress bringing much satisfaction in the next life, depending on how we handled each tasks.

Once we return with a new life contract, we are responsible to remember our purpose by resolutely paying attention to our passions and soul desires. Staying connected to the Life Source through our higher self is of the utmost importance. We need direction from a higher perspective to stay on the chosen path. We especially must follow guidance to keep our faith and positive attitude when we begin encountering the obstacles and speed bumps already agreed on, if we are to learn the virtues that our soul longs to master. If we deny our connection to Life Source, which is omnipresent for us from birth, we might give in to depression and despair which might lead to addictions, aloofness, loneliness and maybe suicide.

Along the way, we are in charge of keeping our vessel in perfect order and balanced physically, mentally, emotionally and spiritually. Friends from our soul family will join us on the journey to be teachers, sometimes through pain, sometimes through compassion and unconditional love. We must remember that it is all in our life agreement. Pets will also come and go to teach, support and love us without conditions. It is that simple unless we forgot where we came from and why.

It is that simple unless we forgot where we came from and why.

When the Earth journey comes to an end, hopefully we will feel complete, grateful for all we have accomplished and received. We will then welcome crossing over as a happy celebration and conclusion of another mission well done. Until then,

LOVE FREELY LIVE FULLY

LOVE freely, LIVE fully and make your life SPECTACULAR!

ACKNOWLEDGMENT

I have a deep gratitude that words can hardly express for many people in my life. I sincerely believe that if I had never crossed path with my beloved rebirthing therapist, Paula Rowe, I would not be alive to tell my story. Coincidences brought me to her 29 years ago and she gave me a new lease on life. How can I ever express enough gratitude to you, Paula?

I am deeply thankful for every person who participated to the making of this book.

Eight years ago, six of my talented medium students said 'yes' to a crazy project of mine. For weeks, they took time to sit in front of me while I was channeling and asked questions for hours, on the chosen subjects of the book. Without them, this book wouldn't have been born.

LOVE FREELY LIVE FULLY

It all began with my best friend Debra who never ceases to ask questions; tons of them! You would think that as a medium, I continuously play Sherlock Holmes. No, I am not curious at all. I ask when someone needs the information, but for myself, I stay pretty much in the now.

Debra, I want to thank you for being my support and giving me the space to bloom and further my spiritual work. Thank you, my precious friend and soul sister for believing in me and cheering me on rain or shine. Thank you also for patiently keeping all of us on track.

For our angel Florence, thank you for often being quieter than a church mouse, but being so attentive that your questions would always take us onto a different perception of things.

Jennifer was the youngest, so loved and so accurately connected to the Life Source that she brought invaluable information to the group. Katarina was the grounded and logical part of the group and with such a sense of humor that would light up the space and everyone in it.

Janella's uplifting disposition and warmth always made us grateful for her soothing presence. Simone is a published writer who fanatically researched to know and understand more. With her joyous energy, she was the sunshine in the group.

A very special thank you goes to Rico Figliolini for giving me amazing guidance and hope about this book when I was giving up on ever publishing my words.

I want to extend my gratitude to a student and cherished friend of mine. Della made time to edit this book, using her years of expertise and her patience. Thank you for the gift.

I wish to tell Stephanie how grateful I am for hours and days spent with me trying to make sense of the words. Also, a huge thank you to Kathy Borrus who graciously edited my book early on, it was extremely appreciated.

LOVE FREELY LIVE FULLY

My mentors are teachers and friends whom I admire and aspire to be like for different reasons. Some are crossed over and some are alive and guiding me to this day.

My most adored mentor is Edgar Cayce who died in 1945. On a spiritual level, we met 23 years ago. He changed my life, opened all the doors of the unknown for me, and our friendship and partnership is everlasting. I know that he shares his wisdom with many people on the planet and I am one of them. I am very lucky.

I am forever thankful to the Master Souls who are highly evolved entities, some having been in the human body, some who are forever directing me from a higher dimension.

I would not feel complete and so strong without the unconditional love, compassion and support of Archangel Michael, who has been and always will be my guiding light, counseling and advising me, making sure that I stay on a humble lightworker's path. Thank you.

ACKNOWLEDGMENT

A man stole my heart two years ago and made me the happiest woman in the world. Carlo is my husband, my inspiration, my loving and patient teacher and my everlasting support in all that I am and all that I do. I can't imagine my universe without his presence and wisdom. I thank God every day for the gift of him and hope to always deserve his love.

The knowledge and understanding that I have acquired through the last thirty years as a mediumship counselor has been a life PhD for me. It has been possible because loving and trusting people gave me the opportunity to help them through hundreds of readings. Thank you for allowing me to be of service to you. I have the greatest job in the world!

Johanne Rutledge Figliolini
Mediumship counselor

ABOUT THE AUTHOR

I am 66 years old and I had my share of tribulations. Sexual abuse from the age of 6 months to 15 years old by my biological father and sexual abuse and rapes from my half-brothers beginning at age 8 and the list goes on. I became a single mother at 17 and had only myself to count on. What saved me was an indestructible faith in something bigger than myself. Nonetheless, I experienced anger,  resentment, a deep desire for vengeance and multiple suicide attempts.

LOVE FREELY LIVE FULLY

I tried multiple forms of therapy but none of them explained 'why' it happened to me, 'why' I was in this body and this life dynamic. I wanted to know 'why' I was born if life was only a succession of painful hardships. It truly made me believe that I was a rotten human being, deserving all that had happened to me. I was convinced that love could never set foot in my life and dying seemed the only way out. As I kept praying for strength, I also kept praying to die.

Life has a way to show us the right path when we stop giving up and choose to push forward. In my early 20's I realized that I was able to communicate with deceased people and I had had encounters since I was a child. It was a scary path to embrace although the gift of a lifetime.

Forty years on this path, brought amazement, knowledge, and more love than I thought possible into my life. This book was channeled because of beloved masters and amazing souls from the other

ABOUT THE AUTHOR

side, who volunteered to answer basic inquiries about life.

For me, to understand where I came from, why I chose to be on Earth and what is the purpose of being alive lighted up my world. As I went deeper in the meaning of life and death and discover the power of being connected to The Source, I no longer felt like I was hopelessly wondering the planet. It took years of pushing forward and I finally landed into a life that I love and my purpose to helping others filled me up with joy.

Johanne Rutledge

Mediumship Counselor

www.reachingsouls.biz

Made in the USA
Coppell, TX
02 December 2020